CAMBRIDGE LIBRARY COLLECTION

Books of enduring scholarly value

Religion

For centuries, scripture and theology were the focus of prodigious amounts
of scholarship and publishing, dominated in the English-speaking world
by the work of Protestant Christians. Enlightenment philosophy and
science, anthropology, ethnology and the colonial experience all brought
new perspectives, lively debates and heated controversies to the study of
religion and its role in the world, many of which continue to this day. This
series explores the editing and interpretation of religious texts, the history of
religious ideas and institutions, and not least the encounter between religion
and science.

The Way, the Truth, the Life

Fenton John Anthony Hort (1828–92) gave the Cambridge Hulsean lectures
in November and December of 1871. First published posthumously in 1893,
with minor revisions, these lectures are built around a sustained meditation
on John 14: 5 – 6. They represent Hort's defence of the continuing relevance
of Christianity in an increasingly science-focused world where religion was
no longer the sole arbitrator of 'truth'. These lectures are a direct response to
the development of Historical Criticism and the aftermath of the publication
of Darwin's *Origin of Species* (1859). Hort argues that confidence in the
'truth' of Christianity can only lead to a championship of science and other
non-theological methods of inquiry for ultimately 'all knowledge ministers
to the knowledge of the highest'. Hort's lectures are a key work of Anglican
theology addressing the issue, still pressing over a century later, of religion's
relationship with science.

T0371465

Cambridge University Press has long been a pioneer in the reissuing of out-of-print titles from its own backlist, producing digital reprints of books that are still sought after by scholars and students but could not be reprinted economically using traditional technology. The Cambridge Library Collection extends this activity to a wider range of books which are still of importance to researchers and professionals, either for the source material they contain, or as landmarks in the history of their academic discipline.

Drawing from the world-renowned collections in the Cambridge University Library, and guided by the advice of experts in each subject area, Cambridge University Press is using state-of-the-art scanning machines in its own Printing House to capture the content of each book selected for inclusion. The files are processed to give a consistently clear, crisp image, and the books finished to the high quality standard for which the Press is recognised around the world. The latest print-on-demand technology ensures that the books will remain available indefinitely, and that orders for single or multiple copies can quickly be supplied.

The Cambridge Library Collection will bring back to life books of enduring scholarly value (including out-of-copyright works originally issued by other publishers) across a wide range of disciplines in the humanities and social sciences and in science and technology.

The Way, the Truth, the Life

The Hulsean Lectures for 1871

FENTON JOHN ANTHONY HORT

CAMBRIDGE
UNIVERSITY PRESS

CAMBRIDGE UNIVERSITY PRESS

Cambridge, New York, Melbourne, Madrid, Cape Town, Singapore,
São Paolo, Delhi, Dubai, Tokyo

Published in the United States of America by Cambridge University Press, New York

www.cambridge.org
Information on this title: www.cambridge.org/9781108007016

© in this compilation Cambridge University Press 2009

This edition first published 1893
This digitally printed version 2009

ISBN 978-1-108-00701-6 Paperback

EX UNO VERBO OMNIA
ET UNUM LOQUUNTUR OMNIA.

FROM ONE WORD PROCEED ALL THINGS:
AND ONE IS THAT WHICH IS SPOKEN BY ALL
THINGS.

DE IMITATIONE CHRISTI.

THE WAY THE TRUTH THE LIFE

THE WAY THE TRUTH THE LIFE

THE HULSEAN LECTURES
FOR 1871

BY

FENTON JOHN ANTHONY HORT D.D.

SOMETIME HULSEAN PROFESSOR AND LADY MARGARET'S READER
IN DIVINITY IN THE UNIVERSITY OF CAMBRIDGE.

Cambridge and London
MACMILLAN AND CO.
AND NEW YORK.
1893

PREFATORY NOTE.

THE fragmentary Introduction which was begun by Dr Hort in 1872, and continued at two later dates, gives in part the history and scope of the present volume; but the revision indicated in the opening paragraph was not completely carried into effect. The first two Lectures were set up in slip in 1872, and after careful revision were passed for press at the close of 1874. The first four sheets were printed off (pp. 1—80), the remainder of Lecture II. remained in slip, and pencillings on the copy suggest that some enlargement of the conclusion was in contemplation. The third Lecture has been printed partly from the original MS. (pp. 95—107; 146—8), and partly (pp. 108—146) from a MS. of later date[1].

[1] This Lecture was delivered on Sunday, Dec. 10, 1871, the crisis of the illness of the Prince of Wales, and the following words were added at the close of it:

This life of Christ, as manifested first through death and then in His Resurrection, may well fill our thoughts to-day, when we have present before us the possible ending of a life dear to us in itself, and doubly dear as having bound up in it much that belongs to the inward life of the nation. Let us earnestly believe that here too, whether by life or by death, Christ the Saviour will save. If He saves by life, let us give Him thanks. If He suffers death to come to pass, let us be assured that He is preparing a more glorious resurrection in the future.

The fourth Lecture has been printed as it was originally written. The MS. has not received any later additions, but something appears to be wanting on p. 166. The 'Notes and Illustrations' were taken from collections made for the Lectures and for the revision of them, and will serve in some measure to illustrate the wider range which was designed for Lectures III., IV. (p. xxvii.)[1].

---

[1] The MSS. of Lectures III., IV. were prepared for the press by the Rev. J. O. F. Murray, M.A., Fellow of Emmanuel College, who also selected and arranged the Notes and Illustrations, and provided the sections of the analysis which are enclosed in square brackets, and passed the whole work through the press.

A few words enclosed in square brackets ([ ]) have been introduced into the Lectures, but no other changes have been made. In the Notes some changes have been made to complete the form of the sentences ; and one or two phrases indicated as provisional in the MS. have been enclosed in half-brackets (⌈ ⌉).

Since I examined somewhat closely the materials available for the volume before they were placed in Mr Murray's hands, I may be allowed to express my grateful sense of the care and judgment with which he has fulfilled a difficult and delicate task. The debt which Dr Hort's friends owe to him is not less because his labour has been a glad offering of reverence and affection to a master.

The title of the Lectures was not finally determined. 'I wish' Dr Hort wrote to me in 1871 'we could have had some talk about the title. I can think of nothing better than "the Revelation of the Way". It is not quite adequate, but it avoids some objections which I should make to others more obvious. No title single in form and simple in language could express the drift of the whole. It seems impossible to go beyond slight indication.' I do not remember that he ever recurred to the subject.

The Ordination Sermon referred to in the Introduction has been reserved for a volume of Sermons for which there is ample material.

These simple facts and dates tell their own pathetic story.   The work, and especially the latter part of the work, was done under great pressure.   'I have not 'touched [Lect.] III.' (Dr Hort wrote to me on Dec. 1, 1871) 'since I saw you...I have worked incessantly, 'despite less favourable health, and have only this 'moment finished No. II.   Indeed I have still to do 'the cutting out...The result now is 90 pp. and I 'fancy I must cut out 60.'

It happened that Dr Hort had accepted the office of Examiner for the Natural Sciences Tripos in the year of his Lectureship, and the Examination came at the same time as the delivery of the Lectures.   In a postscript to the letter which I have just quoted he says, 'Natural Sciences Tripos all next week; Class list 'on the day after the last Hulsean.'   Meanwhile also the anxious question of a removal from St Ippolyts to Cambridge, soon afterwards most happily settled, was under consideration, and the work of the Revision of the N.T. was going on.   It was no wonder then that on Dec. 28th Dr Hort wrote to me: 'I fear it will be 'some [time] before I get over the pressure of these last 'weeks.   It is unlucky, for much home work presses in 'its turn.   Yet'—the qualification is most touching— 'there is also a satisfaction in that combination of 'the Natural Sciences Tripos and of Revision with the 'Hulseans.'

The work was done under great pressure, and the standard of perfection which Dr Hort set before

H. L.   *b* himself made revision and the writing of the Notes, which he considered necessary, more and more difficult. Yet the task was never laid aside. As on many former journeys the sheets and the MSS. were taken to Switzerland on his last journey in 1892.

But while the Lectures in their present form do not represent completely the writer's ideal treatment of the subject, they are, I think, most thoroughly characteristic. To many they will be a revelation of a new side of a many-sided nature. They·are chapters in the history of a soul of singular sincerity, subtlety and depth. They bring the reader who ponders their measured words into living fellowship with one who has known what it is to search for the Light and to see it. They become, like the words of a friend, springs of thought. Every page bears the impress of reality, of breadth of sympathy, of absolute loyalty to truth.

From first to last the living man speaks to us. He speaks 'as a learner to learners' (p. xxxiv.), claiming no finality for his own opinions, and desiring not so much to convey conclusions as to invite fellow-students to enter on the paths which lead to wisdom, 'to en-'courage and aid independent energy of heart and 'mind' (p. xxxv.). He tells us from experience how one inquirer has found the truth, and not merely how he thinks it is likely that others may find it. He turns aside from special kinds of evidence for the Faith to its general correspondence with what we can

discern of human nature and creation. He seeks
'to confront the truth with personal life and know-
'ledge' (p. xxxvi.). He develops the great saying of
Tertullian : *testimonium Deus habet totum hoc quod
sumus et in quo sumus.* He insists on a principle
which is commonly forgotten, that the evidence for
the highest truth 'is to be found in the light which it
'brings, far more than in any light which it receives'
(p. 11 f.).

Dr Hort was better qualified than most students
to dwell on this aspect of the Gospel from the variety
and thoroughness of his own acquirements. From
very early days the keen pursuit of different branches
of 'humanity', of physical science, of history, of
philosophy had familiarised him with a sense of the
interdependence of things and of the unity of knowledge. A passage from his earliest printed Essay in
which he describes Coleridge has been most justly
applied by Dr Moulton to himself: 'with him, as with
'every one to whom truth is more than a subject for
'speculation, there is no line of separation between
'the different subjects of his thoughts, still less be-
'tween his thoughts and his life' (*Cambridge Essays*,
1856, p. 294). With this conviction he shews how 'an
'endless future is opened for knowledge and devotion'
when once 'the truth of God in Christ Jesus is firmly
'grasped as truth': how the Christian faith, as founded
on truth, is the only sure protection against idolatry :
how the knowledge of all things 'is folded up in the

b 2

'knowledge of Christ', and how Christ is 'the way of 'God in human history'. He rejoices in the growth of knowledge, and dwells on the gains and perils of our recent advances 'in the knowledge of the lower 'world'. He brings out under many forms and in many applications that the primary message of the Gospel is the message of life. Everywhere he points to the Incarnation as the supreme fact in which development finds its law, progress its goal, the individual—the fragment—consummation in a Divine unity.

But the strength of personal conviction never interferes with Dr Hort's scrupulous fairness of exposition and argument. In the boldest assertion of personal responsibility he recognises a legitimate place for authority. In the frank acceptance of the obligation of independent inquiry, he leaves room for the salutary influence of tradition. He proposed to himself and to others truth and not victory as the one satisfying aim of debate. And truth was something not to be received only, but mastered and known and used. He reminds us that we shall understand better what Christianity is, when we remember that in this 'the knowledge of truth was for the first 'time set in its proper place as necessary to sound 'life and rightful action.'

So far I have endeavoured to speak of the Lectures as a precious contribution to modern Theology, indicating, as I believe, to those who will seriously study their lessons, how wavering faith may best be strengthened and every treasure of knowledge and wisdom made contributory to the interpretation of the Gospel. But to me they are much more. They are voices which speak to me of an uninterrupted friendship and close intercourse of more than forty years, first in the revision of the Greek text of the New Testament, and then in the work, especially the Theological work, of the University. Such a fellowship, so long, and so intimate, involving from first to last almost incessant discussions of principles and details of criticism, of policy, and of teaching, is, I fancy, without a parallel. I cannot attempt to measure or analyse what I owe to it. It was to me a constant inspiration and strength to watch in my friend the enthusiasm of research, the dignity and power of silent and sustained effort; to be constantly reminded of the necessary harmony of the greatest and least things; to be lifted towards an unattainable ideal, which presents an exhaustive investigation of the minutest details finally issuing in the establishment of the most comprehensive conception of a whole. The strain of such labour might indeed at times appear to be too intense and continuous. No relaxation was admitted except a change of subject. If I not unfrequently pleaded for what I ventured to call proportion in the treatment of some subordinate point, Dr Hort would laughingly reply that 'all life 'was a question of proportion,' but he remitted nothing of his almost microscopic labour. Again and again I have shrunk from asking his opinion on a point of controversy, because I knew that I should not receive simply the unpremeditated answer which I wanted, but should probably give him occasion for a fresh and thorough investigation of all the facts involved in the inquiry. He held, and he acted on the conviction, that nothing was too little to be done as well as it could be done. No trouble, no postponement of his own work, was reckoned of any account, if he could help a fellow-student. He was instinctively jealous to guard the influence of others and not to use his own. He might have produced more if all this had been otherwise. But then he would not have been himself. As it is he has revealed his power and thoughts to those by whom he was not personally known in representative works on textual criticism, on historical theology, and in these Lectures, if I may use the phrase, on divine philosophy; and those who knew him best would, in the words of Dr Phear, not ' wish him to have been other than he was.'

The history of these Lectures will have shewn what painful difficulty Dr Hort often found in formal composition. It was not so in correspondence or conversation. Keen, fluent, fertile, subtle, he raised point after point in a discussion, and where he failed to convince, at least quickened a fuller sense of the manifold bearings of the question in debate.

We met for the last time in the summer of 1890 in this house, dear to us both alike as the home for ten years of our common friend Bishop Lightfoot, and his last resting-place. We talked of what the great scholar had done at Cambridge and the great bishop at Durham : of the new work which had been most strangely committed to me at the close of life : of the work which remained to be done at Cambridge towards the fulfilment of old designs which we had cherished for enterprises at home and in the Mission Field. And where much seemed to be shadowed with anxious uncertainty, one thing I recognised with unqualified joy. Dr Hort felt at length that he was truly known by those among whom he had laboured without one thought of self for nearly twenty years, and looked forward to the future with confident hope, conscious that he should be strengthened for every duty by the eager and reverent affection of younger men. The hope was amply justified by two years of happy and varied activity continued without intermission through failing health. One of his last acts was to accept from two Cambridge scholars (the Rev. J. Armitage Robinson, B.D., Fellow of Christ's College, and now Norrisian Professor of Divinity, and Mr M. R. James, M.A., Fellow of King's College) who could speak as representatives of the new generation, the dedication of an edition of 'the Gospel 'according to Peter and the Revelation of Peter.' Before the book was published he had passed to his rest; and a Postscript, which I cannot refrain from quoting, tells what Cambridge felt:

> It was not without expressions of misgiving that we had asked to prefix to this hurried work a name which must always be connected with the minutest accuracy and the most cautious utterances. It is quite unworthy to be dedicated to his memory. But we feel that we cannot draw back or alter now. As here, so there, his gentle spirit will 'make allowance for us.' To his voice we had looked forward as the one voice which should tell us, as no other could, where we were right or wrong. Now we must learn it in a harder school. But it will remain a sacred duty to carry out these investigations with the patience and deliberateness which his example enjoins and his removal has made more than ever necessary.

A life so lived, however prolific in literary achievements, is more fruitful by what it is than by what it does. It is not lost when it ceases to be seen. It passes into the spiritual atmosphere which sustains the highest life. It confirms by a fresh testimony the belief in the unity of truth and being by which our ancient Universities are enabled to welcome and assimilate every increase of knowledge with untroubled joy. In times, when we are distracted by rival cries or overwhelmed by transitory sorrows, it helps us to 'win our souls by patience,' according to the promise of Christ which reveals to us the way and the end of faithful service.

B. F. DUNELM.

AUCKLAND CASTLE.
Sept. 15, 1893.

ANALYSIS.

LECTURE I.

THE WAY.

LECTURE II.

THE TRUTH.

LECTURE III.

THE LIFE.

H. L.   c

LECTURE IV.

'NO MAN COMETH TO THE FATHER BUT BY ME.'

INTRODUCTION.

THIS volume chiefly represents the Hulsean
Lectures delivered before the University of
Cambridge in November and December 1871. The
first and second lectures are printed substantially as
they were first written, the parts omitted in delivery
being restored, and the whole being revised, with
occasional expansions. The third and still more the
fourth lectures were originally written with difficulty
under physical depression, and fell far short of their
intended scope: in their present form they are to a
considerable extent new. A vain hope of finding
some space of undistracted leisure for recasting them
altogether has held back publication; but the delay
has already been too great. A sermon preached at
the Trinity Ordination in Ely Cathedral on June 15,
1873, is appended to the Lectures: though addressed
to a very different congregation, it may illustrate
some of the thoughts which they are intended to set
forth.

According to the design of Mr Hulse his Lecturer had two duties, to be performed in different courses of sermons; to show "the truth and excellence of Christianity," more especially by "collateral arguments"; and to explain "some of the more difficult texts or obscure parts of the Holy Scriptures, such as may appear to be more generally useful or necessary to be explained." Recent legislation, while curtailing the number of lectures, and abolishing the requirement of publication, has likewise removed these conditions of subject matter. But a combination of the two purposes of the founder was in complete accord with what I held to be the true view of Christian Evidences. For the same reason the restrictions imposed by fitness for the pulpit there had an advantage of their own: it is only in speaking to Christians that a Christian can in any measure set forth without distortion the weightier grounds of faith.

The office was undertaken with some hesitation. Not to speak of various doubts arising out of the responsibility incurred, long cherished habits of mind imposed restraints which made it impossible to desire unreservedly the position of an apologist. Truthful and deliberate vindication of the greatest of all causes, itself truthfully and deliberately espoused, could never be otherwise than honourable, and might in its season be necessary: the flimsy prejudices to the contrary, a word on which may find place further on, could have no binding force over conscience. Yet there

was no gainsaying the often-avowed experience that
Christian truth never appears so vulnerable as after
the reading of treatises written expressly in its defence: and further, a student accustomed to find
truth oftener persecuted than upheld by powerful
majorities, unable moreover to accept some of the
most widely current modes of presenting Christian
doctrine, might reasonably shrink from becoming a
public champion of a dominant and popular religion.
On the other hand, within the greater world of pro-
miscuous sentiment and opinion there is a lesser
world, not wanting in an imperious domination and
popularity of its own, whose presence can be as little
forgotten by anyone who has profited, and desires
always to profit, by contemporary movements of
knowledge and speculation.   The prevailing attitude
assumed of late years by what is called educated
opinion towards the supernatural foundation and the
practical authority of Christian faith has heightened
the responsibilities of Christians who are thankful to
live in a time of free mental activity, and rejoice in
many of its results to themselves and others.   An
attempt to give expression to personal convictions
through an exposition of a comprehensive passage of
Scripture might be expected, it seemed, to escape
some of the dangers of a formal treatise, and to
suggest thoughts favourable to independent belief.

The manner of treatment thus adopted has led of

necessity to an appearance of indefiniteness which
may easily be misunderstood. These lectures abound,
I cannot but fear, in an indefiniteness which is pure
loss, the result of defects in my own thought and
speech. But they have likewise an apparent indefiniteness which I do not regret at all, for it is
inseparable from purposes distinctly contemplated
throughout. Two of them have been already indicated, the expression of personal conviction and the
furtherance of independence in belief. A third, still
more essential to the whole plan, is the appeal to
the relations between the Christian revelation and
the sum of experience, rather than to any separable
and separated credentials. Each of these purposes
requires some˙explanation.

I. The impulse to give the discussion of Christian
evidences an argumentative shape proceeds from a
right source, a sense of the untrustworthiness of beliefs
founded exclusively on cravings and sympathies, and
still more of the difficulty of conveying these grounds
of assurance to others. But this well founded desire
to be rational leads easily to the suppression of personality as inconsistent with an impartial balance of
judgement. Not to speak now of the personal factor
which must enter into every perception of comprehensive truth, the effort to be impersonal affects
injuriously the discussion of Christian evidences to at
least this extent, that it beguiles Christians into
setting forth the considerations which ought, they

think, to be convincing to others, with little or no reference to what has actually exerted power over their own minds. This vicarious or dramatic pleading cannot escape unreality, except where either its scope is negative, that is, the dialectic refutation of objections, or it is dealing with literary or historical or physical phenomena on a purely literary or historical or physical footing: and consequently it can have no final persuasiveness except towards those peculiar minds whose own beliefs or disbeliefs are formed or retained exclusively within these same limits. With or without good reason, most men who seek foundations on which to build a conviction on grave subjects, not excuses for adhering to an opinion, find no help in arguments which, however honestly urged, bear no trace of having proceeded from an actual experience of help already needed and found.

And yet it is no light task for anyone, at least for any defender of a hereditary creed, to follow consistently the more effectual course. Many intelligent and accomplished Christians, of whom it would be a gross calumny to say that they have given no candid study to the criticisms of adversaries, have yet never outgrown the attitude of simple defence. They have tried and found wanting the floating arguments for disbelieving the creed which they have received : but they have forborne to ask for themselves whether it has a supreme intrinsic claim to be believed. Again, this common frame of mind, often justifiable and even right in itself though a source of weakness in vital controversies, is far from being the only obstacle in the way of expounding personal belief. The clearest conviction of the need of independent verification opens no royal road to the fulfilment of the desire. While we are in the region of formulated dogmas, tradition and evidence may be discriminated with tolerable facility: as soon as we penetrate to the underlying region of first principles, tradition often simulates evidence, and evidence tradition, because they are closely intertwined in fact. There are but two ways of avoiding the intricacy of the investigation, both very broad roads, both leading ultimately to perdition; the way of openly or covertly renouncing evidence, and the way of investing the more palpable and tractable part of evidence with the name and authority of the whole. Not least, finally, is the difficulty of expression. Everything personal, —personal thought even more than personal feeling, if the distinction is possible,—is in a measure absolutely inexpressible; and further is relatively inexpressible by reason of the complexities and gradations which distinguish vital from artificial structure. What can be presented is after all not so much the personal conviction itself as a tentative exhibition of some of its leading lines, not detached from the evidence but as perceptible through the evidence. Other modes of discussing these themes have obvious attractions, and have their uses too. I wish only to make it clear how my own aim has been to render account of such results as I have myself been able to attain; and that, if I have anywhere deviated into other courses, the deviation has been involuntary.

This seems to be the fittest place for one other personal statement. These prefatory remarks, intended to elucidate the purpose and necessary limitations of the lectures which succeed, fall naturally into a somewhat neutral tone, of which the free use of such a word as 'problem' may serve as an example. The two modes of speech are, it seems to me, complementary to each other; and I should have been loth to put forth the lectures in the new form of a book intended to be read, without at the same time forestalling misconception by giving independently and in contrast some clearer expression to antecedent processes of mind than the proper character of words preached would allow. Here therefore the language of enquiry is deliberately employed, both because it is by contemplating the controversy under the form of a problem that truth, whatever that truth may be, seems most likely to be attained, and because any essentially different language would misrepresent the manner in which, by a habit which I have neither the power nor the wish to change, the whole subject presents itself to my own mind. Experience fails to confirm the supposition that a matured and assured belief on a speculative subject is incompatible with frequent and fresh reinterrogation of the facts and relations of facts which apparently sustain or contravene it, under the impulse of the new facts or relations of facts which either general or individual progress of knowledge and thought is continually bringing into view. To have become disabled for unlearning is to have become disabled for learning; and when we cease to learn, we let go from us whatever of vivid and vivifying knowledge we have hitherto possessed. At all events it is only as a learner to learners that on these high matters I can desire to speak.

II. A writer who endeavours to speak from his own experience can have little desire to affect his readers except through the medium of experience won in like manner by and for themselves. He cannot pretend to minister to the demand for transferable arguments to silence inconvenient questions without or within. Impersonality of reception is for all great issues as unprofitable as impersonality of speech. In the one case as in the other there is a region within which neutrality and detachment are in place: the unravelling of sophisms and the exhibition of misrepresented or misinterpreted external facts in their true light may render a true and salutary service without the intervention of any further exertion than what is required for the understanding of what is said. But beliefs worth calling beliefs must be purchased with the sweat of the brow. The easy conclusions which are accepted on borrowed grounds in evasion of the labour and responsibility of thought may or may not be coincident with truth : in either case they have little or no share in its power.

What is written with a view to being simply assented to and adopted has advantages of definite form and result denied to what is written with the hope of encouraging and aiding independent energy of heart and mind. This is the hope which has governed these lectures ; and if they do not suggest more questions than they answer, their intention is not fulfilled. I could not willingly be instrumental in supplying ready nourishment to the credulity which is truly said to be a dangerous disease of the time. The vast multitudes of simple Christian people who know no difficulties, and need know none for themselves, are of course not in question here. Fundamental enquiries constitute no part of their duty ; and though the exemption disqualifies them for some among the higher offices of service to their fellows, it leaves them perhaps the more capable of others, according to the Divine allotment of various responsibility. But the easy belief, the easy disbelief, the easy acquiescence in suspense between belief and disbelief, which infect those other multitudes upon whom the burden of asking themselves whether the faith of the Church is true or not true has been laid, are manifestations of a single temper of mind which ought to cause Christians more disquiet than the

growing force of well weighed hostility. Owing to
the deceptiveness of words credulity is popularly
imputed to those only who land themselves on the
Christian side; though the same impatient indolence
of investigation, the same willingness to choose and
espouse or neglect evidence in obedience to proclivi-
ties of outward association, may lead equally in
different temperaments and circumstances to any one
of the three positions. But it is from the credulity
of Christians that the Christian faith suffers most in
days of debate; and it is well when any who might
have helpfully maintained its cause among their
neighbours, had they not been disabled by too facile
acquiescence, are impelled to plunge into the deep
anew.   There is not indeed and cannot be any
security that they will emerge on the Christian side :
in human minds truth does not always win the present victory, even when it is faithfully pursued. But
whatever be the present result to themselves or to
others through them, it is not possible that they or
that any should fall out of the keeping of Him who
appointed the trial : and to the Church any partial
loss that may arise is outweighed by the gain from
those whose faith has come to rest on a firmer foundation.   Truth cannot be said to prevail where it is
assented to on irrelevant or insufficient grounds ; and
the surest way to evoke its power is to encourage
the strenuous confronting of it with personal life and
knowledge.

III. The preference for personal efforts of apprehension as the base alike of speech and of reception
of speech depends ultimately on the true nature of
Christian evidences taken as a whole. The problem
of Christian evidences is immeasurably simplified by
neglecting either the credentials or the contents of
the Christian faith; and thus it is not surprising that
controversy has for the most part oscillated from the
one topic to the other, partly in mere reaction from
the preceding stage of controversy, partly in direct
accord with the philosophy prevailing at the time.
Each mode of simplification is however bought by
the suppression of essential fact, and a clear recognition of the complexity and wide range of the
problem is the prime condition of its successful
solution.

*   *   *   *   *   *

Βογληθεὶς ἀπεκγήσεν ἡμᾶς λόγῳ ἀληθείας, εἰς τὸ εῖναι ἡμᾶς ἀπαρχήν τινα τῶν αὐτοῦ κτισμάτων.

Of His own will He engendered us by a word of truth, that we might be a kind of firstfruits of His creatures.

ST JAMES.

Χριστοῦ οῦν παθόντος ϲαρκὶ καὶ ὑμεῖϲ τὴν αὐτὴν ἔννοιαν ὁπλίϲαϲθε, ὅτι ὁ παθὼν ϲαρκὶ πέπαγται ἁμαρτίαιϲ.

Christ therefore having suffered unto the flesh, equip ye also yourselves with the same mind, for he that hath suffered unto the flesh hath ceased unto sins.

ST PETER.

ἐν ᾧ εἰϲιν πάντεϲ οἱ θηϲαγροὶ τῆϲ ϲοφίαϲ καὶ γνώϲεωϲ ἀπόκρυφοι.

In whom are all the treasures of wisdom and knowledge hidden.

ST PAUL.

Λέγει αὐτῷ Θωμᾶς
Κύριε, οὐκ οἴδαμεν ποῦ ὑπάγεις·
πῶς οἴδαμεν τὴν ὁδόν;
Λέγει αὐτῷ Ἰησοῦς
Ἐγώ εἰμι ἡ ὁδὸς καὶ ἡ ἀλήθεια καὶ ἡ ζωή·
οὐδεὶς ἔρχεται πρὸς τὸν πατέρα εἰ μὴ δι᾽ ἐμοῦ.

H. L.   I

THOMAS SAITH TO HIM
LORD, WE KNOW NOT WHITHER THOU GOEST:
HOW KNOW WE THE WAY?
    JESUS SAITH TO HIM
I AM THE WAY AND THE TRUTH AND THE LIFE:
NO ONE COMETH UNTO THE FATHER SAVE THROUGH ME.

JOHN XIV 5, 6

LECTURE I

I AM THE WAY.

THE Gospel in all its parts and all its forms makes provision for the infinite future by giving answer to finite questions already asked. The same character is stamped on the written records in which it is conveyed. There too human search precedes Divine revelation. The words of our Lord belong more to dialogue than to discourse; and it is seldom possible to arrive at their principal meaning while they are treated as solitary aphorisms, without a history, and therefore without a purpose. The definite fitness with which they were first spoken is the measure of their lasting power, and even of their universality.

On the other hand few if any of the questions addressed to our Lord received an answer in the shape that was desired. It is not enough to say that His merciful wisdom withheld such replies as might have proved injurious to the moral state of

the questioners. The replies which He gave were
not merely more profitable but more true, and more
apposite in their truth, than any others could have
been. It is an idle fancy that to what seems a clear
and positive question there must needs be some-
where a clear and positive answer of pure truth.
The necessity exists only for the most abstract or
the most concrete things. All questions in which
the spiritual realm has any part contain within them
assumptions in thought and in word; and these
assumptions cannot but be more or less affected
by human infirmity. An answer which tacitly
ratified all assumptions would convey substantial
falsehood under at best the form of truth. Its
barren show of justice to the question would involve
injustice to the questioner.

For every questioner who is not the merest
sophist, if indeed we dare make that exception,
is concentrically manifold, self within self; and the
question which alone he is able to present in words is
but a rude symbol of the question in his mind, as this
again is but a rude symbol of the whole search within.
The verbal question is not for that reason slighted
or condemned by the Divine answerer. Its very
imperfections belong to it as a necessary part of
that perpetual seeking which is the condition of all
progress and therefore of all spiritual life. But His
constant aim is less to give present satisfaction than
to seize on the present demand as an opportunity

for initiation into a future and progressive satisfaction, to be vouchsafed to ripening powers and expanding knowledge. Every question has some relation to the universe of truth; and the truest answer is that which best conducts from the one into the other.

Among the questioners in the Gospels, who stand in various positions towards the Lord as He moves in the midst of them, the chief place is held by those called Disciples or learners. They saw in Him, as did others, both the Teacher or Rabbi and the Lord or Master. What distinguished them from others was the clearer, fuller, and so to speak more personal sense which these conventional titles assumed in their minds and on their lips. The teaching and the ruling which they received entered deeply into their hearts, and awoke new activities within them, which in turn bound them faster to the Teacher and Lord. As discipleship grew stronger, the personal and comprehensive relation almost absorbed the more external and partial relation; the Teacher was for the most part forgotten in the Lord. The single outward act by which the inward character of discipleship was signified is following: the command "Follow me" included all that came after. He passed along the way as the head of a company: His disciples were with Him and yet behind Him. There were various degrees of adherence among those who were thus attracted out of the indifferent multitude. Some continued disciples for a shorter or a longer time, and then walked no more with Him. Others were still holding fast to Him when the last evening of His earthly life closed in.

The supper of that last evening was eaten with the twelve who were called the Disciples by preeminence, disciples in whom the character of discipleship was most fully shewn. The Lord had chosen them out of the general body of His disciples with a double purpose, as St Mark distinctly tells us, that they might be specially attached to His own person, and that He might send them forth out of His immediate presence as heralds and envoys to distribute His word and power. In this second capacity He named them apostles, and sent them forth at once on a prelusive apostolic mission. But their apostleship was not and could not be a promotion out of discipleship. After their mission they became disciples more than ever. They understood more clearly what it was to be disciples, and entered on a higher stage at once of intimacy and of dependence. The accession of apostleship involved the perpetuity and the increase of discipleship.

From the Last Supper and the incidents which accompanied it discipleship to the Lord received its permanent consecration; and from the words which were then spoken till the departure into the garden its articulate interpretation. In the upper room in the midst of the crowded city the disciples were assembled together alone with the Lord, that they might learn how to find their way in the outer throng. They were lifted for a season on high apart from enemies and neutrals and even other disciples, that when they resumed their place among their fellows they might not be dragged down by the world which they were appointed to raise up.

Judas had gone out. The glory of the Son of man, and of God in Him, had been announced. Then the Lord, presiding at the table as the head of a family, recalled the affrighted Eleven to themselves: "Little children," He said, "yet a little while I am with you." These first words of tenderness, reaffirming the bond of their life which had seemed to be falling to pieces, prepared them at the same time to hear of that change in the form of their relations to Him which was to be the starting-point of His remaining teaching. He declared it in words that for the moment placed these His beloved disciples beside the hostile Jews of whom He had said that they should die in their sins: "Ye shall seek me, and as I said to the Jews, Whither I go, ye cannot come, I say to you also now." He passed on at once to give a new commandment, the foundation for which was only now completely laid, but the necessity and stringency of which would soon be grievously apparent; the commandment to prove the reality of their discipleship by bringing forth its proper fruit, that is, by loving one another. If they had been intelligently

receiving into themselves the love which He had been
pouring forth upon them with this very end in view,
the breaking of the bond hitherto provided in His
visible presence would leave them still endowed for
holding together on a common course, still true representatives of Him to mankind.

Here first the disciples broke in with their questions. St Peter, foremost as usual, impatient of the
unexpected commandment which seemed to him to
be a wandering from the engrossing theme of the
discourse, brought back the naked fact of departure :
" Lord, whither goest thou ? " He received for answer
the double assurance that he could not follow now,
but that he should follow afterward. Again he
flung aside the promise of the future, and demanded
the reason of his inability to follow instantly, profess-
ing his readiness to suffer death for his Lord. His
dream was still of an individual discipleship and an
individual martyrdom, in the pride of which he was
too willing to draw himself away from his fellow-
disciples, and to forget altogether the world which
he had to help to save. The personal testimony
proffered after this fashion was itself fallacious: it
argued a self-knowledge so slight and delusive that
that *Why* was of necessity asked in vain. One
season of probation was indeed over, but another
with sharper searchings was already coming into
its place. The sifting as wheat had as yet scarcely
begun.

After this first interruption the Lord took up His
discourse again in words of peace. A distrustful
alarm had arisen at the outset when it was declared
that one of the disciples should deliver up the Lord,
while each feared himself and feared every neigh-
bour. It must have taken a new but hardly less dis-
turbing shape when the sop disclosed the mind of
Judas, and the circle of the Twelve was broken. It
could hardly be dispelled even by the tenderness of
the language conveying the tidings that the Head
Himself should presently depart from among them.
Accordingly He now began with bidding their heart
not be troubled; and as He had before taught love
among themselves, so now He taught faith, faith
resting on God and on Himself. Then He returned
to the subject of His departure, shewing how its
nature and purpose justified the two-fold faith, and
converted the seeming abandonment into a fresh
token of attachment. The separation, He explained,
was intended to lead to future reunion on a
higher stage; and meanwhile it was no disappear-
ance into darkness: "Whither I go, ye know the
way."

Again the question of a disciple gave a new
turn to the discourse. But this time we hear not
personal impatience but calm sensible bewilderment.
"Thomas saith unto Him, Lord, we know not
whither thou goest: how know we the way?" It
is almost as though it were an argument speaking

rather than a man. Yet the argument was no
mere sophism: there was a genuine perplexity
within, and it arose out of an existing difficulty.
The unwillingness to forego the use of reason,
even when it weighed in the balance the Lord's
own words, was not an impulse that the Lord
could simply rebuke. The desire to try the truth
of what had been received was a gift needed for
His disciples no less than the eagerness of St
Peter. Each quality had to be brought into
subordination to the supreme faith, that it might
be purified from base admixtures. It needed to
be cultivated and trained, but in no wise to be
extinguished. And so the answer given to St
Thomas in the first instance was not a personal
expostulation but the statement of an universal and
unchanging truth: "I am the Way and the Truth
and the Life; no one cometh unto the Father save
through me."

The universality of announcement proceeds here
as elsewhere from fitness of answer. The discourse
throughout receives its form from the peculiar circumstances of the hour: it looks back to the last
common meal which has just been eaten, and forward
to the separation which will have begun before the sun
rises. But the teaching demanded by the hour has
been leading the thoughts of the disciples downwards
and inwards to a wider range of contemplation and
a truth which is independent of times and seasons.

"Whither I go ye cannot come." Why? Because "I go my way to make ready a place for you." How? Seeing that "I am the Way and the Truth and the Life"; and that "no one cometh unto the Father save through me." Within the threefold saying itself there is the same movement downwards and inwards towards what is most fundamental and comprehensive as in the preliminary steps which have led to it: "I am the Way" as being the Truth; "I am the Truth" as being the Life. Then in the last clause there is a return to that idea of going, now changed to coming, on which the verse is founded; and the three preceding announcements are gathered up in terms of the first into a single statement which is in form a negation. But a further step is simultaneously taken: by the culminating utterance of the Father's Name the one ultimate goal of the one journey is announced, whither Christ Himself goes, and whither He brings all that has been given into His hand.

These four declarations of Christ provide us with ample materials for study on four successive occasions. Each has its own distinct sense, while each would be barely intelligible without the aid of the others. In the four together is expressed the Christian view of human existence as beheld in one primary aspect. The truth which they combine to set forth is not one of those lesser truths which can in any sense be either proved or disproved. Its evidence is to be

found in the light which it brings, far more than in
any light which it receives.

Thus far we have been endeavouring to apprehend in outline the historical position which must be
held steadily in view in any attempt to interpret
rightly the three-fold and four-fold revelation of Christ
and of all things in Him.   The next step is to consider the immediate sense of His first word concerning Himself: and for this purpose we must
examine more closely the contents of His preceding
exhortation to faith, which had been interrupted by
the question of St Thomas.

The new call for faith arose out of the impending
separation between the Lord and the disciples.   Yet
the separation was in fact directly involved in
the journey or passage which He was making
throughout His earthly life.   If it was a real journey,
and not an aimless wandering, it must have a definite
beginning and a definite end.   For us this beginning
and this end are laid dqwn by the Evangelist in
the weighty sentences which introduce his narrative
of the last evening, when he refers the Lord's
acts during the supper to His knowledge that the
hour was come that He should pass from this world
unto the Father, and again to His knowledge that
He came out from God and was going unto God.
But this comment of the Evangelist dates from a
later retrospect.   As yet no such declaration had

been made by the Lord to the disciples, who were
desiring to keep Him with them in the world. To
the unbelieving Jews He had spoken of His 'going';
and once to the officers sent by the chief priests
and Pharisees to catch Him, that they might expel
Him from the world, He had said, "Yet a little
while I am with you, and I go unto Him that sent
me." But this idea of a return home from a mission
abroad is changed for another now when He is
speaking peace to His own disciples. The character
in which He speaks is not that of an envoy but
of a Son ; and the earth itself is no longer a distant
or foreign shore, but lies within the heavenly precincts:
the interval remains, but it is subordinated to a
mightier comprehension. He calms the tumult of
the disciples' hearts by pointing to the wide compass
of His Father's house. In one of its 'mansions', its
abiding-places for the stages of the journey, He and
they are reclining and speaking. His departure would
be only to another abiding-place within the same vast
house ; or at least to what would be to them another
abiding-place though the word should cease to be
appropriate as applied to Himself. He speaks not of
another place to which He is going, but of going His
way that He might prepare a place for them, that where
He is they also may be. Thus in what He says
of His own journey He keeps out of sight all distinct
images of locality ; and even when He refers to
their journey to come, He at last resolves the place

to be prepared for them into a simple sharing of His presence.

By these words, "that where I am, ye also may be", He had led them back at once to the ground of their dismay and to the single sentence in which He had first recalled them to a true sense of the crisis; "Little children, yet a little while I am with you." Their fear was that they were about to lose that which as yet they possessed, that is, the being with Him; and so He taught them that their being with Him was itself a purpose of His departure. As yet it was hardly possible for them to feel the difference between His being with them where they were, and their being with Him where He was. That He should be with them where they were had been the necessary commencement of His work; and they naturally craved perpetuity for that state, the only manner of His presence with which they were hitherto acquainted. But their craving, the form of their desire, must needs be disappointed if the substance of their desire was to be fulfilled, and if Christ's own work, which coincided with the substance of their desire, was to be accomplished. It was indispensable that He should take them unto Himself that so they might pass to being where He was. That was the transition now coming into sight in His person, the transition from a presence taking its character from their circumstances to a presence taking its character from His. In this thought the

end of His impending journey was sufficiently expressed for the immediate need. The particulars of
its progress, more especially of its later issues, must
remain unknown to the disciples. But the Lord
instantly reminded them that they had by this time
the means of ascertaining the direction of the journey
from that portion of the road which was already
manifest to them. In all that had met their senses
or minds or hearts during their discipleship, and in
all that was in prospect now, not unillumined by
prophecy and vision, the requisite knowledge was
already given. "Whither I go, ye know the way."

St Thomas in the question which he interposed
had clung literally to the figure. The conditions of
locality which the Lord used freely and discarded
freely, as symbols of a truth which could be only
symbolically conveyed, became to the disciple the
entire reality. In his eyes the journey must be like
one from land to land or, as we might say, from
planet to planet. It was certain that neither he nor
his fellow-disciples knew to what spot of space the
Lord was going: how then, he asked, could he or
they know the road, the way, by which He would
have to travel? He detached the single phrase from
all that led up to it and illustrated it. The words of
encouragement which he had heard uttered in the
same breath went for nothing. He had no ears for
the faith that was to calm down the troubling of
heart, or even for the promise of reunion.

Such at least was the character of his verbal
question, the question which admitted of no answer.
Yet beneath this literalism of speech there must have
been, in him and in the others, a sincere perplexity
at the readiness with which the Lord faced the
apparent cutting off of His work, while as yet it was
apparently little more than begun. And again there
was evidently a still stronger perplexity about the
future which awaited a disciple of Christ. He could
not forget that when he followed Jesus of Nazareth
he had been drawn away from his old life and placed
in a new life. Probably there was no wish to turn
back; but there was a helplessness as to what was to
be done next. He had been leaning on the personal
direction of Jesus; and he had no perception now
of what was to come when that personal direction
should be withdrawn. The inherited ways of Galilean
custom had already lost their sufficiency. That impalpable but potent guidance which we all derive
from the ways of men around us, from their usual
thoughts and feelings and habits, mingling on the
one hand with what he had received from his parents
and forefathers, and on the other with the lesser
variations made by the details of his own individual
life before the preaching of John,—all this had ceased
to be helpful now. The Master's voice had taken its
place: how was he to shape his course when the
Master's voice could no longer be heard?

Thus the inward doubts of the disciples, so far as

they are represented in St Thomas, were at least
two, the announced separation being the occasion of
both. They desired to know both whither their Lord
was bound, and also what they were themselves to do
when He was gone. The former of these questions
alone found utterance in St Thomas's words. But the
Lord, who perceived the current of his thoughts, met
both questions at once by an answer which seemed to
take account only of that which had not been uttered.
The way hitherto mentioned was the way which He
was Himself to go: the way which He now declared
was the way which His disciples were to go: "I am
the Way";—the Way in every sense; for thee, and for
all the Eleven, and for all my disciples, and for all
men.

Here lies at once the difficulty of the passage and
the key to its meaning. A true answer could not in
the nature of things be given to either question without the other. On the one hand the way of Christ
in His own person, so far as it can be known to us,
is inseparable from the destiny of those whom He
draws to Himself. On the other hand no one can
discern a true way for himself except so far as he
discerns it in relation to an universe of greater ways
which all meet in one Divine Way. The way of man
is known only so far as the way of God is known.
To learn by experience the identity of the two ways is
to learn the supreme lesson of life.

If this strict interpretation of Christ's saying is

H. L. 2

difficult to grasp through words, yet no other will either account for the association of the Way with the Truth and the Life, or accord with the historical position. The inadequacy of some obvious dilutions of the sense will appear as soon as they are examined. First, Christ could not mean "I shall still and always be your Guide." There were two reasons why He should neither say nor mean this. He would have seemed to be promising a continuance of just that order of things which was coming to an end ; whereas His purpose was to wean the disciples from the habit and need of recurring to an external leader as the sole director of their motions. But further, He was about to speak to them of another Guide whom He would send to them from the Father, one whose guidance should be after a different manner from His own, adapted to the new stage in their training, while leading towards the same end. He could not promise still to be their guide, without confusing their thoughts about that other Paraclete, whom it was needful that they should recognise as clearly as they recognised Himself.

Nor, secondly, would it have availed for Christ to call Himself here the Example. The word will bear a true and innocent sense ; but only in proportion as it is removed from the idea of a model and brought near to the idea of a way. "Whither I go," He had assured St Peter, "thou canst not now follow me, but thou shalt follow me afterward." More distinctly

on a former occasion He had said, "Take up my
yoke upon you,"—the yoke which I carry,—"and learn
from me." But passages like these go far beyond
imitation. Even under the peculiar circumstances
of the previous discipleship imitation had always
been subordinate. In so far as Christ had been the
Example to His disciples, this character had been
but one part or aspect of His relation to them as
Teacher, and His teachership one part or aspect
of His relation to them as Lord. In the coming
time these relations would continue, but transformed
and on another scale. The marvellous expansion
which Christ's lordship would undergo would affect
all which it included, His office as Teacher and as
Example. The work begun by Him was to be
carried on by those who had learned from Him; but
it was to be carried on under every variation of time
and place and circumstance. Each act of true
apostleship would lead further away from the original external conditions, and render more indispensable the interpretative office of the Spirit. The
outward fashion in which the Lord had shewn Him-
sel would be profitable only according as it was
studied as the means of coming to know Himself,
His work, purpose, and character, nay His nature and
being. No remembered or recorded incident of His
life in the flesh would be without its store of instruction concerning His perpetual kingdom. Yet imitation of Him in the strict sense would be always at

2—2

once a delusion and a retrogression. Knowledge of Him after the flesh must give way to knowledge of Him after the spirit.

It was therefore impossible that Christ should mean "I am the Guide" or "I am the Example" when He said "I am the Way." Those phrases may exact a slighter effort of thought; but only because they belong at best to a rudimentary and transitory form of truth. It was doubtless hard for those who reclined around that table to understand in what sense one in fashion like themselves could say "I am the Way". Perhaps it is equally hard for us who have received Him through the Creeds in His Divine majesty. Whether spoken from the human lips of Jesus or from the highest heaven, the words have a perplexing sound which no Jewish forms of speech suffice to make clear. They must always remain unintelligible as applied to the function of a simple Teacher or Ruler. The claim which they embody includes not merely a set of men moving in a world but the world itself which contains them. They convey a doctrine of Creation and Providence, not merely of historical mission; a claim on the part of the speaker to permanent supremacy in the whole manifold economy of circumstance. They are the practical and ethical expression of an all-embracing truth which we may perhaps apprehend best in the form of two separate doctrines; first, that the whole seeming maze of history in nature and man, the

tumultuous movement of the world in progress, has
running through it one supreme dominating Way ;
and second, that He who on earth was called Jesus
the Nazarene *is* that Way.

From the absolute meaning of the words we pass
on to their verification in the earliest Christian experience. They were spoken in the upper room at
Jerusalem to men trembling between the old and
the new, overpowered with the mingled sense that
they were committed to something indefinitely great,
and that He on whom they depended for light and
for strength was withdrawing Himself from them.
They were spoken by One who knew alike the hearts
of His disciples and the mission on which He was
sending them. As He knew the exact nature of the
need, His words must have been directed towards
supplying it. It was to action that He had called the
disciples, and so the teaching which they needed
now must be helpful towards action. If they were
to receive and publish a belief, yet it must be a
belief which should kindle to action in themselves,
and perpetuate and multiply the impulse and the
enablement to action in those who should receive
it at their lips.

Now that which most palsies the heart and the
limbs for action is the doubt whether there be any
true 'Way', any line of coherent purpose designed
and achieved either in our own lives or in the larger

sphere of the world without. No doubt this is a palsy which implies some measure of serious reflexion: it is only too easy to escape it by being beneath it, if it is hard to rise above it. A blind immersion in the pleasure or profit of the hour, or even the sedulous pursuit of some private and capricious 'way' which may sometimes be accomplished by reason of the nearness or pettiness of its scope, will often be sufficient security. But it could not be so with the disciples, not even with a Judas. Their eyes, once partially opened to the kingdom of heaven, could never be quite closed again. Henceforth it must be either believed or not believed or both at once: it could not be sunk out of remembrance. A necessity lay upon them of either seeing a divine way in their own lives and in the course of things around, or of being wretched and helpless because they could not see it.

The belief in the existence of such a 'way' belonged to the disciples before the ministry of Jesus or the preaching of the Baptist; for it had descended to them by inheritance from their forefathers. They had received it moreover not as an abstract proposition about human affairs, from which the existence of a disposing God might be inferred, but rather conversely as involved in the ancient faith in the Lord God of Israel. The germ of it was contained in the faith of Abraham: it came to them enlarged by each lesson of the ancestral history. The Psalter instructed them for the most part in the way of God as it had become known to many an Israelite in the sum of his personal experience, that life of his which was entirely his own and which gave him his individuality. The Prophets on the other hand, and some of the later Psalmists, had discerned and depicted for them the way of God chiefly in the fortunes of their race and the wider concourse of nations. In the past history of mankind the way of God, so far as it was visible, was visible as embodied in Israel; and so far as it had been recognised, had been recognised by Israel. In this as in other respects the Twelve were endowed with the gifts of the Old Covenant.

But if the disciples were no strangers to the idea of a way of God in either the inner or the outer region, it may well have been with them, as with others, that the faith accepted was fading into a hollow tradition of what it was proper and seemly to believe. All things within and without were tending to dissolve the ancient faith. The thoughts and ways of other nations had for a considerable while been creeping in among the beliefs and customs of the Jewish past, and it was vain to exclude them. There was light of some sort in them, and who could refuse the light? Yet it proceeded from no potent and unwavering source, but from a vague disorganised decaying world of thought and impulse. It shewed that the time was come for new growths of the old truth, but it was destitute of power to inspire them

or to govern them. Even those who came in no
direct contact with the dissolving influences proceeding from the Gentile inundation, which was overflowing Israel, found it harder than the men of old
time had done to trace the Divine footsteps in
themselves or their people or the nations without.
Individual devotion was no longer sustained by the
proud and joyful feeling of citizenship in a city at
unity with itself. Thrown back on its own resources,
it shrank and wasted and came nigh to doubting
whether what had once been thought to be the way
of God was more than the figment of a too ingenious
piety. The outward signs of it in truth were such as
it was difficult for a simple Jew to recognise. The
course which the world was taking, and, worst of all,
the increasing debasement of the chosen race, might
well seem to make a way of God in the destinies of
mankind altogether incredible.

The needed assurance came at last when the
Gospel came. But if it was to be effectual to assure,
it must needs do more than assure. A late repetition of
the revelation granted to Psalmists or Prophets would
have been of little avail, even for restoring that which
was decayed ; and far more than this was needed.
In order to preserve and restore, it was necessary
to advance. But the advance in the knowledge of
the Way of God was itself at once that for which
the wants of the time most urgently cried out,
and for which the counsels of God had hitherto been

preparing. The Cross, the Tomb, and the Mount
of Ascension, taken in conjunction with the works
and words which had preceded and accompanied
them and the descent of the Holy Ghost which
followed them, not only lighted up the Way of
God on earth but laid bare its foundations in the
Way of God in the heavens. The fixed relation and
action of different 'Persons' within the Godhead,
and the age-long working out of creation and redemption in accordance with that fixed relation of
Divine 'Persons', were revealed as underlying all
the movements of created things. The Lord of the
disciples was found to be the Sole-born Son of the
Father. That which He was as manifested to His
chosen, including equally that which He did and
that which befel Him, was at once the perfect image
of human destiny and the perfect image of the Divine
Counsel; the Way in man, if there be any Way in
man, and the Way of God.

Again, as the disciples found Christ to be indeed
the Way, when they looked for a Way in relation to
God, so they were led by personal experience
to a like result through recognition of Him as the
Way for themselves, according as they sought for
guidance in their own lives. While we consider the
subject only as curious spectators, students of a
world that is not our own, the idea of Christ as the
Way for a handful of weak and shortlived mortals
will appear to be separated from the idea of Christ

as the universal Way of God by an impassable chasm, and each will carry an air of unreality. But in experience the one is found to lead to the other. When the word was first pronounced, the disciples must have received it chiefly as spoken with reference to their own goings; that is, as an intimation of the manner in which the Lord in the fixed past and the unchanging eternity and the ordained future might to themselves take the place of the Lord whom they had hitherto known only in a series of ever changing presents. But the habit of believing in Him as the Way laid down for themselves, and of walking in Him accordingly, would more and more turn their thoughts from their own feet to their task itself and its purpose, and so to the dealings of God with mankind, and the part therein assigned to Christ and discipleship to Christ. Thus, not by a verbal fancy but by the operation of the Divine order in which human nature has its being, the words of Christ would by degrees be filled out with the loftier sense suggested alike by the language of the prophets and the contemplation of a world-wide mission. Christ the Way would now mean Christ the Way of God in human history; the Way sought after and recognised and followed, however imperfectly, by all who strive to choose freely that which God wills; and the Way along which the Almighty leads His unwilling no less than His willing hosts slowly on towards the distant end.

This necessary expansion of the individual Way into the universal Way was likewise involved in the characteristics of Christ's own earthly existence. At first sight the departure might not unnaturally be identified with the whole journey, and the journey be conceived as a simple transit from point to point, in which the way itself would be of no account except as a means of swift arrival at the end. This negatively individual conception of the way as affecting only him who moves along it, if the disciples had been allowed to acquiesce in it, would have not merely narrowed but inverted their faith, and the purpose which their faith was meant to inspire. Had they learned to believe that the following of Christ which still remained for them meant simply their own arrival with more or less ease and speed at a distant haven of rest, the greater part of their past experience would have been vain. No earnestness of endeavour to lead others into the same purpose, however fruitful in blessing to themselves and to all who listened to their message, would have saved them from the inward contradiction which accompanies the working out of a conception in itself radically untrue. When Christ said "Whither I go, ye know the way," He was pointing not merely to the goal but to the portion of the way already traversed. The departure was a critical stage of the journey, but it was not the whole of it, and it could not be understood by itself. His journey through human life, as already known, was not as that of one who speeds on his lonely course regardless of the land which he is traversing. He passed on not as through a wilderness where all is ownerless and homeless save the thread of way itself, but as through His heavenly Father's domain; wherever He trod, He took possession and exercised sovereignty in His Father's name. And so the way which He left trodden in the earth, the way which is Himself, was not a means of flight from a strange and hostile waste, but the token and the instrument of universal Divine lordship and therefore of universal Divine care and use. It was the high way, the way which bore witness to the King's authority, and gave free movement as well as guidance to the King's servants when they went forth to do His work or came home to His presence. The disciples who followed Him in such a way, or walked in Him as such a way, were by it brought into relations of intercourse and affection with all that surrounded them, while they were at the same time led to see it stretching forth into all ages and all worlds.

Such was the actual experience of the disciples. We do not see it all in process, but we do see it in result. The written memorials of their faith, which they have left behind from various stages of its growth, bear unimpeachable witness. The pregnant use of the single phrase "the Way" in the Acts of the Apostles cannot be adequately explained except by their clear insight into this character of the Lord and

His office. In the other writings the phrase itself almost disappears; but only because the idea which it represents, in conjunction with other ideas of the same order, has been transfused into infinite renderings, and has determined the whole structure of primitive Christian thought and feeling. All later forms of Christian doctrine, starting from a more partial and limited conception of Christ's relation to human action, while they find in the Apostolic teaching many echoes or reflexions of themselves, find also in perplexing abundance unexpected turns and combinations of language which they can interpret only by explaining them away. This strange language is for the most part the expression of instructed faith in Christ as the Way, or it may be as the Truth or the Life. It is the native and proper language of that part of the Christian heritage which came neither from Jew nor from Gentile but from the Gospel alone. Like all other language it may be caught up and repeated with conscious or unconscious unreality. But so far as it expresses a full and sincere conviction, it is the language of consummate discipleship.

The Lord spoke the word : the disciples tried it and found it true. In the power of it they discovered that decisive and resolute action was open to them after He had ceased to be visibly in their midst. Weakness, suffering, shame, death abounded to themselves : delay, disappointment, decay, failure abounded to their enterprises. But they came to know that all

were merged in Christ, buried with Him in His death
that they might rise to a better life. Every excuse
for devotion to their own lower or higher welfare was
nullified, when they saw that the ordering of all
events in heaven and earth was conformed to the
image of that heavenly Redeemer who had emptied
Himself for their sake. None could serve His person
who yielded only an unwilling service to His kingdom. Yet the weight of the world's future rested not
on their shoulders but on His. They had but to be
faithful to Him, to His work and to His mind; and
they were rewarded by becoming partakers of His
sorrow at the human sin which they ever shared, and
of His joy at each human victory over evil, whether
they had themselves been agents in it or not.

He was Himself their Way: while for their
guidance for walking in it they had the promised
Spirit. He supplied in Himself the fixed plan according to which all right human action must be
framed: the Spirit working with their spirit supplied
the ever varying shapes in which the one plan had
to be embodied. Utter obedience to the Father's
will, utter love of the brethren, and the utter sacrifice
of self which is the constant inward condition of both,
remained to all eternity the substance of every human
greatness, as they had been shewn to be the powers by
which the Son of God fulfilled the work committed
to Him alone: while the wisdom of the Spirit's teaching cast them again and again in ever new moulds.

The way on which the disciples went forth in due season to conquer the world has been handed down to us for our instruction as regards the most essential points. During their lifetime the march of events was rapid, and the end might almost seem to have broken away from the beginning. Not less various among one another were their temperaments and manners of thinking, or the tasks which fell severally to their lot. At each step they had to deal at once with the perishing ruins of local custom and religion, through which the several nations had unconsciously performed their respective tasks in the great preparation, and with the shamelessness among the evil, and the aimlessness among the good, which followed the lapsing of the old ways into worse than primitive savagery. Yet the more deeply their acts and discourses and letters and visions are investigated, with patient discrimination and comparison of each difference of work and teaching, the stronger grows the conviction that throughout they together trod one way themselves, and by the treading of their feet left one way indestructibly impressed on the earth for the Church, and therefore at last for mankind, for evermore ; and that that one way was no other than the One Incarnate Lord Himself.

The experience of those disciples was in one sense unique. That outward and sensible discipleship of

theirs was necessary once for all, to be both the unfad-
ing image of spiritual discipleship and the foundation
of the written records which were to make it possible
hereafter. But the question of Thomas and therefore
the answer of the Lord repeat themselves incessantly
on the largest and on the smallest scale. There is
a discipleship of the Church itself, the living representative of the chosen company around the table
of whom St Thomas was but a spokesman. There
is also a discipleship of the individual Christian, who
may find a likeness of himself in one or other of
the original disciples. Both the Church and the
Christian have to pass through seasons of crisis not
unlike that evening spent in the upper room, Divine
probations, in which faith not seldom sinks and
perishes, but which have been given for the renewal
and enlargement of its powers. By considering the
trial of these two forms of perpetual discipleship in
turn, we may be able to learn in what manner Christ's
word "I am the Way" is still and always a revelation
of vital truth.

The eve of the Passion is not the only time when
Christ has seemed to His Church to be departing
from the earth of which for a while He had been a
denizen, and when those whose course has been in
great part shaped by the discipleship to Christ which
surrounded them have felt with dismay that the
sustaining habitudes were passing away. His own

palpable presence in the flesh has its counterpart, at least as regards the sense of security which it afforded, in a 'Christian world', an assemblage of nations where deference to His Name and acquiescence in His authority receive full public and private recognition. When it becomes manifest that a Christian world in this sense is ceasing to exist, either because Christ's authority is becoming limited to a single narrow department of individual life, or because His right to authority is questioned altogether at its fountain-head, then the band of His disciples may naturally feel as though He were once more leaving them to themselves. They cannot go backward: if discipleship has not yet taught them the Way, it has at least disabled them for ever for resting contented without a Way, and convinced them no less that elsewhere it is not to be found. Yet it is hard to see either whitherward the Lord is departing or after what manner the original command to follow Him is henceforth to be obeyed.

The one sufficing encouragement, the encouragement which comes with clearer vision and surer guidance, is provided in the answer of Christ to St Thomas, illustrated by the primary experience of which the books of the New Testament are the monument. As He who had been leading a chosen few along a way which He shared with them revealed Himself in that hour as the one universal Way, so the same revelation, when understood and embraced in its full breadth, delivers His Church from helpless

dependence on any partial tokens or recognitions of
His guidance. It beckons onward not to some laxer
and feebler form of allegiance to Him as safer and
more lasting; but to a faith in Him, and in the treasures hidden in Him, both deeper and wider, in itself
and more complete in its mastery over our whole
nature, than any to which we have yet attained.

It is not ill but well for the Church that some
temporal and external characteristics which marked
the time of probation and apprenticeship should
vanish, even though we can scarcely distinguish their
loss from the loss of Him to whom for long centuries
they have borne witness. If He takes away any
familiar signs of His presence, it is because they are
becoming hindrances to the ripening of discipleship.
New knowledge of Him has to be learned: new works
for Him have to be undertaken. It is His own voice
which bids us 'arise and go hence', that we may find
Him and follow Him elsewhere.

It is a progress and a gain to the Church to have
to consider how much is involved in learning Christ
as the one Way which was from the beginning; to
have to study therefore in the Gospel the lineaments
of the Son of Man with a care and comprehensive-
ness which were not possible to earlier generations;
and on the other hand to have to discern and follow
the Way not only as He is manifest in the chosen
body which bears His name, but as He abides hidden
in the wide outlying universe of human action and

knowledge. So only can it fulfil its task of moulding in secret the future of human welfare.

Moreover the Church has for its guidance a fresh accession of knowledge of the Way not shared by the original disciples. It possesses its own experience as they possessed and bequeathed theirs. The history of the Church from its foundation to the present hour is hardly less necessary to the Church at large than the Gospel itself, whatever it may be to the individual disciple. For the Church now to enquire concerning a Way for itself, without study of the Way as revealed in its own history, would be as though the apostles had stripped themselves of the memories of what they had heard and seen and looked upon and handled, by way of preparation for going forth among the nations. "Have I been so long time with you and yet hast thou not known me?" Such is the language in which we may still hear our Lord recalling us to an undervalued and imperfectly used experience. Doubtless for the Church, as for the first disciples, what lies before differs widely from what lies behind: but that which runs through both alike is the One Way, the same yesterday today and for ever; to be traced alike in the successes and in the failures of the past, and to be followed unflinchingly through whatsoever unlooked-for windings it leads among the unfolding hopes or fears of the ages yet to come.

And therefore once more it is a progress and a

gain for the Church to have to go forward in the
Spirit, making experience that the Guide sent by
the Son from the Father will never fail to hallow, to
unite, and to enlighten the body which is bold in
faith to make free use of all its heavenly endowments,
and in faith to draw supplies of needful material from
every quarter, so long as it advances along the Way
which is Christ. For the dispensation of the glorified Christ is also the dispensation of the Holy
Ghost. The Way and the Guide along the Way
were revealed together.

The revelation of the Way to those first disciples
who were also Apostles retains its complete force only
for the Church itself, the universal body to whose
stewardship are committed the mysteries of the
kingdom of heaven. But the faithfulness with which in
each generation the stewardship is exercised depends
at last on the degree in which its members have
severally received the same revelation each into his
own heart, and governed themselves by obedience to
its light. A discipleship of some sort, nearer or
more distant, has been upon us all from the earliest
years; and countless powers within and without are
ever at work to dissolve its bands. It begins, happily
and rightly begins, in tradition and custom: but the
growth of character demands an independent life, and
the inevitable change is a true progress only when
the discipleship of custom becomes converted into

the discipleship of intelligent and willing service, the recognition of the Way and the walking in it.

To us in this place the early years or even months of our stay here precipitate the change in one direction or another. The first long probation is over. We stand in the interval of freedom between the personal subjection of childhood and youth and the fateful bondage of middle life, due partly to universal necessities but still more to the consequences of our own acts. The leading-strings have been severed. A wide and various world lies before us, with a seeming power in ourselves to turn whithersoever we will. At such a time the new sense of liberty well-nigh revolts at the idea of a Way. The delightfulness of the opening world depends in no small measure on its semblance of waylessness. To stray deviously at will over hill and dale, sipping of every fountain, is the almost acknowledged ideal to which we rejoice to be able to approximate.

But in due time the ways of nature and the world disclose themselves, and we find ourselves insensibly journeying along one or more of them, bound by heavier chains of custom without or habit within than any of which we had experience at the outset: and sooner or later the question is heard demanding an answer, what is the end of the journey, or whether it has any end. The choice given us, we then find, was not between wandering or journeying, but between journeying this way or journeying that. This is the

true meaning and purpose of our temporary freedom,
which is no delusion but a happy reality. What we
have to choose then in the days of choice is nothing
less than the character of the bond which is to make
our actions coherent. To every one whose thoughts
of life are not wholly unworthy it is evident that some
bonds of action, some ways, are hateful and that
others are noble. But on the actual surface of things
the forms of nobleness and hatefulness are easily lost
to view in the mixed or neutral mass: and perplexities of various kinds press upon us even when we
bend all powers of thought and will to finding out
some one way which shall as it were include all
other right ways and guide our lives towards the
highest end.

Here again Christ meets us with His inexhaustible
answer, "I am the Way;" and the answer, if it gives
food for lifelong meditation, gives also sufficient light
for immediate action. This power it has wherever
the energy of self-knowledge and self-mastery is not
wanting: and the power increases in proportion as we
learn to bear in mind that we are members of a vast
society, parts of a vast universe. Much may remain
dark to us; but the purposes of life receive a clear
and powerful direction the moment we believe that
the one supreme Way of life is that Jesus Christ,
God's Son, our Lord, who has been made known to
us from the first in the Creed. No other single way,
capable of uniting the whole nature and life of man,

has yet been discovered or devised which does not tend to draw us down rather than lift us up. But if in Him is shewn at once the Way of God, so far as it can be intelligible to man, and the Way of man according to God's purpose, then many a plausible and applauded way stands condemned at once as of necessity leading nowhither; and many a way which promises little except to conscience is glorified with Him, and has the assurance of His victory. Yet, when the primary choice has once been made, the labour is not ended. The Way is no uniform external rule. It traverses the changes of all things that God has made and is ever making, that we may help to subdue all to His use; and so it has to be sought out again and again with growing fitnesses of wisdom and devotion. Thus the outward form of our own ways is in great part determined for us from without, while their inward coherence is committed to our own keeping; and the infinite life of the Son of man can transmute them all into ways of God.

The original chasm between the human question and the Divine answer is not and cannot yet be more than partially filled up. The purpose of the answer is not merely to satisfy our want, but to raise the manner of our thoughts by degrees to a higher level of truth. It stands always above and beyond the experience which it illumines. From the first it sends forth a quickening light; and the light increases as we advance. At each stage we see a little beyond

what we have attained, but never more: fresh insight
comes always and only as the reward of fresh attainment. We can at once believe that various truths
which we now represent to ourselves inadequately in
other forms are all comprehended in the one assurance
that Christ is the Way. But we shall never reach the
full measure of the word till the journey itself is
ended, and with thankful wonder we find ourselves
wholly gathered to Him in the place and presence
assigned from the beginning by the heavenly Father's
will.

LECTURE II

I AM...THE TRUTH.

IN the counsel of God David the righteous was
succeeded by Solomon the wise ; for both characters
had to be combined in the true king of Israel. The
kingdom already set up had now to be consolidated,
administered, and maintained. While the demands
upon what the Bible calls righteousness were greater
than before, righteousness itself could subsist and prevail only by growing to a higher type, and so increasing in subtle complexity of power. The time was past
when rude impulses could suffice: without the constant
enlightenment of wisdom the efforts of righteousness
would be narrow in purpose and poor in result. Nor
was the highest sanction wanting to the advance, for
both characters were already embraced in the faith in
God Himself. As the righteous Lord loved righteousness, so human wisdom came to be regarded as His
requirement and His gift, as soon as His own wisdom
in the creation of the material world and in the ordering of the ways of men received distinct homage.

Though Israel stood virtually alone in its emphatic exaltation of wisdom as a divine virtue, other nations knew how to admire it for its beauty or prize it for its uses. After a while their own progress led them to perceive that wisdom has no independent existence, but lives by knowledge; and that knowledge must become an object of conscious and sedulous pursuit if wisdom is to attain maturity. During three generations of the wisest of heathen nations that belief in the intimate connexion of righteousness, wisdom, and knowledge inspired meditations and researches within the field of knowledge which no imperfections and contradictions can rob of the undying veneration which is their due. Yet for the time the labour seemed to be in vain. Disbelief in the possibility of knowledge and limitation of wisdom to personal prudence soon followed as steps in a process by which righteousness became reduced to an optional luxury of private life for peculiar temperaments. The fruits of the labour were not to be enjoyed by the immediate heirs. The power was not yet born which must sooner or later gather up all the treasures of the nations for the enrichment of mankind.

At length, at the season prepared by the Lord of the ages, the necessity and the sacredness of knowledge were manifested to those who had inherited the slow but irrevocable stages of His revelation in Israel. 'Knowledge' is the word that we naturally use while we are pausing on the human faculty. But the books of the New Testament carry us on past knowledge to the object of knowledge, and prefer to speak to us of 'truth'. The possession of truth is one of the distinctive marks of the new covenant; and so the full and careful use of truth is the distinctive agency by which a ripe wisdom and therefore an effective righteousness is made attainable for Christians. It was no new thing to desire and pursue and find truth. It was no new thing to aim at the service of God as the highest end of action. But it was an altogether new thing to learn that the knowledge of truth is indispensable for the mature service of God, and that the desire and pursuit of truth is an essential part of a holy worship.

By this mark more perhaps than by any other was it signified that mankind, as represented by its foremost members, had passed from youth into adult age. "The law was given through Moses," says St John near the beginning of his Gospel; "the grace and the truth came into being through Jesus Christ." The Law proceeded from the invisible Lord whose character was ascertained by His dealings with Israel and Israel's ancestors: but the lawgiver who promulged it as a mediator between God and Israel was a mere instrument for the special purpose, separate from the Law itself. The Law itself was a code of ordinances: its revelation consisted in specifying this or that act as good or evil by means

of individual rules, and these rules were adapted to
a temporary discipline. On the other hand that which
came through Jesus as Christ was not, strictly speaking,
a newer and better law: it was the grace and the truth
of the Divine order which the Law had shadowed
forth by its decrees.   The relation of the grace
and the truth to Him, unlike the relation of the
Law to Moses, was one of personal embodiment. The
grace and the truth for man came into being and
into manifestation through Him, because He, the
Word become flesh, was Himself full of grace and of
truth, and we did but receive out of His fulness. As
the power in Him was the grace, so the revelation in
Him was the truth. God's people were no longer
merely to hearken and obey, but in the fullest sense
to look with their own eyes and see and understand.
The new exercise of the faculties which had been
long preparing was called forth by the appearance of
the one adequate object.   When the Truth of truths
was shewn, then the study and contemplation of
truth assumed its proper place for the direction of
all human feeling and thought and action.

God's manner of speaking to Israel had never been
purely preceptive or directive. It had always asked
for faith ; and faith by its very nature implied some
tried experience. But the new expansion of faith
required a new expansion of rudimentary experience
into knowledge of truth. As the experience which
came first was real, so the knowledge of truth which

came after was real too. The experience was furnished
by believed facts of history: the knowledge of truth
could not be less substantial. To crown a childhood
of true if crude and slender experience with a manhood
of salutary illusion would be unworthy of a Divine
education. The truth which Christians were called
to know was not a phantom truth, a baseless contri-
vance for generating results of conduct such as would
please God or make men happy. The world without
had already reached a stage in its mental history in
which phantoms of truth abounded ; and this fact of
itself was a mark that the time was come when it
was well that the true truth should be brought within
its reach. When men had once begun to study actual
truth concerning man and nature, to have bestowed
on mankind a merely economic truth concerning God
would have been to make every advance in knowledge
an advance towards godlessness. If the truth contained in the Gospel were not as solid veritable truth
as any other mental possession which we can call
truth, it must have only widened the fatal breach
in the unity of human nature which was making
progress impossible for either Jew or Gentile when
Christ came. The severed personality could be re-
united only by the union of truth with the service
of God. If Christ did not perfect the simple antique
righteousness into a better righteousness founded
on knowledge of truth, then righteousness was already
outgrown. If His revelation of God was not a

revelation of truth, then godliness was a step towards ignorant delusion, and at last towards contempt for righteousness.

It follows next to enquire whether the Gospel itself, as we hold it in our hands, ratifies the claim made on its behalf that it is not merely a salutary announcement but in the strict sense a revelation of truth. Is the claim to be sustained only by constraining a few obscure and isolated texts to bear unnatural service to a foreign teaching; or is it rather the recognition of a dominant purpose which was from the beginning? Was this purpose intimately involved either in our Lord's earthly life or in the faith of the Apostles concerning Him?

The answer to these enquiries can evidently be found only in the letter and spirit of the books of the New Testament themselves. In the first three Gospels the word 'truth' does not occur except in a slight and secondary sense. Nor is the absence accidental: these Gospels do present Christ more expressly as the Way than as the Truth: in outward form they convey rather the disciplinary nurture by which the power of apprehending truth is called forth. No prominent place is assigned to 'knowledge' by name, that is to the apprehension of truth: but its latent dignity and authority are attested by some grave and characteristic passages; as when the Lord tells His chosen disciples that to them hath been given to

take knowledge of the mysteries of the kingdom of
God.

But when, leaving words, we go on to consider the
matter of the Gospel as it is set forth by the first
three Evangelists, and to reflect on the meaning of
the sights and sounds with which they surround us,
we find that their world is indeed a world of knowledge, whatever else it may be, and that to any other
view it remains fragmentary and incoherent. Many
scattered sayings doubtless yield Divine virtue and
illumination to casual and random use, though even
then they perplex by unlooked-for manners of speech
or unlooked-for silences. But the full light shines
from them only when they are beheld as parts of a
whole which must needs be diligently traced out,
signs of a many-coloured and fertile world that lies
beneath. The most characteristic words of the Lord
in these Gospels are the parables; and in most cases
it is hard to feel the peculiar value either of their
teaching or of the form in which it is presented,
except so far as we are able to use them as gates of
entrance into a wider truth, suggestions of God's
hidden ways of administering His creation. They
touch all worlds of which we have any cognisance;
in their language the sky, the earth, and the doings
of men; in their meaning all these, together with
the invisible worlds above and beneath. And ever
in the midst is the form of the Son of man Himself,
having His portion in every world of which He

speaks, and bearing witness to the unity of each and all.

The evidence increases as we pass to His acts. Now we lay stress on their power, now on their beneficence or mercy or love; now we regard them as credentials of Himself, now as testimonies concerning the Father above, whose true Son He was declared to be; and in each case with good reason. But it is impossible to gain a satisfying view of their fewness and their number, their repetition and their variety, their intrinsic mastery and their involution with spoken words, if they do not constitute a lore of positive truth, that is to say, a setting forth of the laws and constitution of that inner order by which all things are fixed in their true places, 'the kingdom of God' or 'the kingdom of the heavens'. And if we are thus constrained to recognise in the simple recital of Christ's ministry of word and deed an intended revelation of truth, we shall at least be prepared to believe that the histories which precede it from the birth of John, and even the unique and transcendent events which close it, the Passion and the Resurrection, partake of the same character, though the first three Gospels may not furnish conclusive evidence to this effect.

It is only however when we open St John's Gospel that the larger function of all the Gospels is disclosed. Assuming a knowledge of such facts and words as the others had already recorded, it brings to light the hidden base which makes them intelligible as objects and as vehicles of knowledge. Each of the three was by itself a sufficient and satisfying narrative of historical occurrences, selected out of existing material, expanded by new material, arranged, worded, under the guidance of a single large but limited purpose. When however the three met together in combined use, it became necessary to shew that they were indeed but three different pictures of a common object. Yet a mere recombination of their elements, with or without additions, into a single new whole would have been a loss rather than a gain. The result would have been an individual portraiture, less instructive than any of the preceding delineations by very reason of its comparative completeness, leaving uncombined and unexplained the distinct forms of office in which they had severally depicted our Lord, harmonising details at the cost of a false and deceptive simplicity. Each separate exhibition of historic truth had been suggestive of an underlying universal truth which was intended to be known. Their proper harmony could never have been displayed in a purely historical record, a biography of Jesus the Nazarene. It could only be reached by a fuller exposition of His historical manifestation as related to theological truth in the strictest sense; and such a complementary exposition, instead of superseding them, would raise them to a higher and a permanent function in the service of truth.

H. L.   4

This was one of the purposes fulfilled by the Gospel of St John, and it is clearly denoted by changes of language. External acts are called 'signs', and thereby marked as eloquent of a corresponding matter of truth. Truth itself assumes a substantive form and is called by its own name. The earlier Gospels had recorded words spoken and deeds done, the full significance of which could not be perceived till the experience of the Apostolic age was complete. There was nothing exceptional in the delay. Much is often said and done from a single design which yet is not at the time expressly. named. Premature naming might be fatal to sound action, and especially to sound discipleship. The lesson itself has to be well learned in various forms before the name is given. But in due time a distinct perception of the common character of what has been learned is needed, at least by those who have in their turn to lead and teach ; and so the name itself is needed as a bond of consistency and permanence.

Thus it was with 'truth'. The word had been used by the Lord on several occasions with striking vividness and yet plasticity of meaning. The last period of the Apostolic age brought into clear light the danger of allowing this character of the Gospel to be forgotten or thrown into the background : and thus St John was led to place on record the Lord's own utterances concerning the truth, as well as to make it a principal theme of his own teaching. In his

Gospel 'the truth' is inseparable from Christ's own work and from the work which He bequeathed to others. It is the truth of God, which He has heard from God and speaks to men: it is that into which He promises that the Spirit of the truth shall guide His disciples; and in which He prays the Father to hallow them. When at last He is called before the Roman governor, the representative of the victorious power which knew how to use and value almost every human possession except truth, He sums up His earthly career in words that remind us how the King of the Jews had His title written up over His cross in Greek letters as well as in Roman and in Hebrew: "Thou sayest that I am a king: I for this cause am born, and for this cause am come into the world, that I might bear witness to the truth; every one that is of the truth heareth my voice."

Before the Roman He stood as it were in allegiance to the truth, chief among its faithful servants and witnesses. He had brought the truth closer to Himself when He was speaking to men who by birth and education were better fitted to understand Him, and had even begun after a fashion to believe Him, though soon they were to be divided from Him by a deeper gulf than heathenism could make. They were those Jews who are said to have believed on Him at the time when He told them that where He was they could not come. To them He said, "If ye shall abide in my word, ye are truly disciples

4—2

of mine, and ye shall know the truth, and the truth
shall make you free." Abiding or continuance in
His word, that is, in those things which having heard
from the Father who sent Him He spake into the
world, would be the distinguishing mark of true discipleship to Himself: personal adherence would be
nothing without resolute acceptance and use of what
He revealed. But further that true discipleship would
itself bear two successive fruits; and these would be
two forms of responsive life within. The privileges of
true disciples of the Lord would be first to know the
truth for themselves, and then to have power to act
from themselves, that power of freedom being bestowed by the truth which they should come to know.

The familiarity of the words hides from us the
singularity of the office here assigned to the truth
and the knowledge of the truth. Freedom of action,
itself not merely permitted but held forth as the culmination of a Divine promise, is made to depend on
knowledge of the truth, and knowledge of the truth is
made to depend on learning from the Son of God.
A learning pregnant with these results could never
mean simple reception of enunciated doctrines or
simple execution of formulated commands. But as
little could it mean simple copying of acts; for what
place would then be left for knowledge? How wide
soever be the sphere of possible free action, so wide
must be the sphere of the truth that has to be known,
and of the knowledge of it. The range of the truth

into which the Lord here promises to give His disciples entrance is limited only by the necessities of
their free action. Wheresoever they have need to
move, there they have need to know, and there He
promises that they shall know. But then what can
He be whose disciples can draw such infinite resources out of their discipleship? As oracle or law-
giver or human model He can contain in Himself the
fountain-head of no such various potency. His own
nature must be so inwardly at one with the nature of
man, and of every world in which man can move, that
in the knowledge of Him must be folded up the
knowledge of all things. He cannot be less than
Himself the Truth.

When Jesus said plainly to the Eleven in the
upper chamber not only "I am the Way" but "I
am the Truth", we can now see that He was con-
densing into a word one primary aspect of all that
His ministry had been implying and all that His
teaching had been expounding in varied phrase. The
trial of discipleship had proceeded far. Many who
had once been attracted to His person had fallen
away by reason of His teaching. During the last
hour the one traitor out of the chosen Twelve had
gone into the darkness without. The boldest of the
Eleven who remained had just been warned that before the cock crew he should deny His Lord. Yet
they are addressed as tried and approved disciples,

whose remembered past of discipleship has already become a possession, which henceforth they will have to explore and employ in every kind of need.

Moreover the apostleship instituted and imperfectly exercised of old among the villages of Galilee is now being confirmed as the crown of discipleship. The time is fast approaching when the learners will be brought into a more perfect and yet a more humbling manner of learning, by finding themselves set to teach. For this end as well as for their own necessities it is no longer enough to possess : they must come to know that which they possess, in order that they may be able wisely to impart.

Hence the teaching of which they are the stewards takes now a more comprehensive shape. That the many single lessons already received may not be scattered and lost for want of insight into the foundation of their unity, the full capacity of language is put forth. Words are pronounced that would be unintelligible if there were no recollections whereby to interpret them, and which can never be perfectly interpreted till the last probation is complete ; but which are nevertheless the indispensable master-keys for the understanding of either past or future, and still more for learning how the past and the future are ordained to be one. To hear the word spoken "I am the Truth" was not to be made the depositaries of a majestic but impracticable enigma. It was to receive at once a fit reward of service already rendered and an en-

dowment with powers to render service of a higher
order.

Thus all that the Eleven had witnessed and endeavoured since the baptism of John bore its part
in enabling them to receive their Lord's identification
of His own person with the Truth. But this revelation had also been immediately preceded by another
identifying Him with the Way, which stood on a
precisely similar footing towards their experience
hitherto. It was the question of Thomas concerning
the way which He was about to take in departing
from them that led Him to declare Himself to be
the Way: and on the other hand the answer was
not merely incomplete but unsustained till the other
and so to speak deeper aspects of His character and
work had been made known. The necessity for the
addition of a second and a third revelation was twofold. It was demanded alike for the sake of human
understanding and by reason of essential fact. The
Way itself could not be clearly apprehended unless
the Truth and the Life were held up simultaneously
to view, so that the contrast might aid in dispelling
the vagueness inseparable at first from ideas of such
magnitude. But the relation was one not merely of
contrast but of dependence. The place which Christ
holds in the movement of events as the Way implies,
if we may venture to use such language, that He holds
a corresponding place as the Truth in the permanent
order of all things that exist. The Way lies most

on the surface as presented to our faculties; further down lies the Truth, and beneath the Truth the Life. It is because the eternal Son of God is the Life that He is the Truth; and it is because He is the Truth that He is the Way.

Although, as we have seen, Christ's manifestation of Himself to His disciples had throughout been such as could not be consistently interpreted unless He were Himself the Truth, yet their relation to Him had belonged mainly to the sphere of action; it had been a following of Him in the way. Their apprenticeship within Israel had borne a resemblance to the experience of Israel itself. They had been advancing from uncultured righteousness towards righteousness founded on knowledge; learning to enter into truth but not yet fully trusted with its administration. But in these last discourses Christ was making known to them the new charge which He was committing to them, and its very nature presupposed a setting forth of new apprehensions of Himself as the satisfaction of new needs of mankind. While therefore His answer was in no word superfluous or irrelevant with reference to their questions, it carried them swiftly beyond the range of their immediate thoughts. Within the limits of the present there was no solution to be found for the perplexity of the present: and the perplexity itself was part of the initiation for the coming form of ministry.

The universal Way seemed barely to touch the single way about which St Thomas had enquired; the Truth seemed to lie remote from it altogether, and to intrude thoughts congenial only to more tranquil hours. But the Divine breadth of true answer, the Divine gift exceeding all the human asking or thinking, went along with the announcement of the new contents of faith and teaching, by which the distinctive character of Christian apostleship should be determined. And further instruction was immediately to follow in Christ's promise that One who would take the place of Himself, a second Paraclete or Advocate, should be sent to their aid.

The distinctive name by which He denotes that other Advocate is "the Spirit of the Truth". He calls Him by this name at the outset; and after once identifying Him with 'the Holy Spirit', repeats it again and yet again. He goes forth, Christ teaches, from the Father, the God who is true, and bears witness to Christ as the Truth. This is the service which He renders to the Truth, as being the Spirit of it; and the witness which He bears does not supersede but involves the witness which the chosen disciples have likewise to bear, as having been with Christ from the beginning. But further this testimony of the Spirit of the Truth to Christ the Truth determines the manner of His guidance of the disciples in the future. As He guides them along the Way, so also He guides them into all the Truth: by faithful following along the Way, they shall be brought within the Truth, and so the Way itself shall take larger proportions as presented to their eyes, and justify itself more clearly to their faith. The Spirit of the Truth shall take up the office of their Teacher, yet not in any wise without Him who has been their Teacher hitherto. Christ has yet many things to say to them, but they cannot bear them just now; the weight of the words is too great for them to carry. But the Spirit of the Truth shall teach them by putting them in mind of all things which Christ has spoken to them. He shall glorify Christ by taking of that which is Christ's and telling it out to them; and as what is Christ's includes all that is the Father's, so whatever can be called the Father's must come within the Spirit's exposition of the Truth. The knowledge of Christ as the Truth shall constitute the substance of all their future learning, while the Spirit of the Truth shall train and enlighten them in the perception and application of it. They who follow the Spirit's guidance will not receive an illumination enabling them to dispense with truth, but the enablement to lay hold of truth: the voice of the Spirit will be heard only in the interpretation of truth, and specially of the Truth. For He shall not speak from Himself. He will utter no independent oracles, making of none effect the fixed and undecaying teaching which is provided in the incarnate Son, or weakening

allegiance to the primary authority of the Father;
for He too, like the Son, shall speak only whatsoever
things He shall hear. Thus on the one hand the
Truth given in Christ will need from age to age His
expounding to unlock its stores; and on the other
hand the faith in Him and His office in the present
shall never loosen men from the Gospel given once for
all, or draw them away from the eternal Father, by
enabling any voice born only of the present to seem
wholly Divine. Standing fast in the unchanging
Truth and an endless progress in taking knowledge
of it shall be indissolubly united.

Yet in another sense the future is specially His.
As He of old had taught the Prophets to read
the future through the past and the present, so
now He shall tell out the coming things to the
disciples. By His guidance the eyes of the disciples
shall be fixed not so much on what lies behind,
though there lies the embodiment of the Truth,
as on the future: and this very pointing to the
future will be indispensable to His mission as the
interpreter of the Truth. For the Way along which
Christ's chosen are led is always an ascent; and
it is only in the light of the future that the most
essential truth can be seen to be truth indeed.

Such are the instructions concerning the truth
and the way of entering into it which Christ addressed to the disciples. In His prayer to the Father
knowledge and truth likewise find a place. The

opening petition discloses the heavenly and, so to
speak, the earthly results of His work ; glory return-
ing through the Son to the Father, and eternal life
given to all which the Father has given to the Son.
"And this," He says, "is the eternal life, that they
know thee the only true God, and him whom thou
hast sent, Jesus Christ." Here therefore 'the eternal
life', the highest form of the highest gift, is made
dependent on a knowledge; the objects of this knowledge being first the Father of Jesus, as the only true
God among many false and phantom gods, and next
He whom the true God sent, the utterance of His
truth. We rightly shrink from identifying such a
knowledge with other forms of knowledge to which
we cannot refuse the same name. Yet not in vain
was the name chosen here. If this knowledge requires the cooperation of faculties which we do not
usually associate with knowledge, the name is not
thereby transferred to an unfitting use : as all knowledge ministers to the knowledge of the highest, so
yet more is it in the knowledge of the highest that
the nature of all knowledge is best to be understood.

The prayer for the disciples turns on their appointed relation to the world. Its various thanksgivings and petitions flow forth from the purpose
declared in a single sentence: "as thou didst send
me into the world, I also sent them into the world."
His Apostleship was to prescribe the function and

the conditions of theirs. Like Him, they should go
forth into the world to overcome it for its own
sake : like His, their mastery over the world for good
would depend on their inner separation from it, tran-
scending the outer commingling: without a secret
hallowing like His they would be powerless to strive
a few against many. But the agency by which Christ
prays the Father to keep them safe apart in holiness
is the truth: "hallow them in the truth ; thy word
is truth." Even such, He evidently means to say,
was the manner of His own mysterious self-hallow-
ing for their sakes. It was wrought by His abiding
contemplation of the things which He had seen
with the Father; and through Himself a hallowing
like His, a hallowing in the truth, would be possible
for them. He speaks not here of sanctity of life,
or fervency of devotion, or unsparingness of labour ;
for though these have a necessary part to play
in the hallowing, yet by themselves they are as it
were blind. The truth alone can prescribe the scope
of the hallowing ; and the study and pursuit of the
truth alone can bring it to pass. Whatever is worth-
less, unclean, unjust, unholy, evil, is before all untrue; the pursuit of it is the pursuit of a delusion.
Christ's life of deed and speech, which is the Father's
word as uttered under human limitations, alone
is free from all delusions: it rests on the perfect
recognition of truth, and truth for man is perfectly
expressed in it. His disciples are safely preserved to

do His work by taking knowledge of the truth committed to their keeping in His person.

The declaration, "I am the Truth", and the succeeding promises and prayer which illustrated it
received a further interpretation in the actual experience of the disciples. In the narrative of what
befel them, the names of truth and knowledge are
rarely heard, because their doings are henceforth 'acts
of apostles'. It is through their dealings with others
that they become known to us; and those with
whom for the most part they had to deal were in
a state which called indeed for a ministration of
truth, but did not yet permit it to be distinctly recognised as truth. Under the primary Apostolate of
Christ they had been themselves brought into discipleship. Now that by the Resurrection and Ascension
His Apostleship had been visibly lost in His Sonship,
the task of their derivative apostolate was to bring
all the nations into discipleship. It was but a pre-
paratory discipline which they administered, analogous to that by which they had been taught themselves. In the final prayer, as already quoted, He
had identified with 'truth' that word of the Father
of which He had said just before "I have given them
Thy word". And so through the book of the Acts,
as in the Gospels and of old time, truth is presented
in this its simplest shape as involved in 'the word
of God' or 'the word of the Lord'. The teaching

of the apostles was founded on what was to their own minds the concrete presentation of essential truth, the Life, Death, and Resurrection of the Lord, and the light thence cast on God's eternal counsel and His plans of dealing with men. As occasion required, they were led to draw forth various inferences: but the truth itself they recognised as subsisting in that primitive condensation of the historical Gospel.

On Jewish soil the function of knowledge under the Gospel could hardly be brought to maturity. That was in the first instance one of the tasks committed to St Paul, himself Jew, Greek, and Roman at once, Divinely admitted to share the apostleship, and Divinely set apart for the extension of the Church beyond its primitive borders. The position which he maintained at Athens in the midst of the Areopagus was more than a personal becoming all things to all men: it was the solemn unfolding of the Gospel as the sanction and the fulfilment of knowledge in the metropolis of the human search for truth.

There as elsewhere in the Greek world the professed study of truth had withered into the idlest of all imaginable frivolities. The kindred appetites for speaking only what was new and hearing only what was new had replaced the old passion for searching into what is true; and as a natural consequence the city was full of idols. One of the altars erected expressly to an unknown god supplied in the two

words of its inscription the fitting text for the discourse in which the apostle of Christ expounded the
faith that was both old and new.   They were the
confession at once of a bastard philosophy and
of a bastard religion.   The restless fear of unseen
powers which was characteristic of all idolatry in its
decay reached its highest point in this superfluity of
irrational awe.   The essence of what we call super-
stition St Paul marked by two corresponding words
of his own, as reverence unaccompanied by knowledge: 'What ye with ignorance revere,– as not knowing it revere,– that I declare to you.'   A religion
which had once possessed some power for good had
come to these dregs, because it was incapable of any
genuine communion with knowledge: it made no
pretence to rest on truth.   So also the pursuit and
hope of knowledge had wasted to a phantom, because
it could not be at once comprehensive and consistent
unless God had a place in it; and the hereditary
religion gave no footing for a Divine knowledge to
be the crown of all other knowledge.   If later speculation, by stretching forth an imagination where knowledge failed, had created for itself a cloudy mono-
theism which imparted some coherence to the contemplation of nature, its hold on the nobler world
of man was feeble and incoherent: in the face of his
sin and his death it had nothing to say.

St Paul encountered the despair of knowledge
and the abandonment to a reckless and baseless

religion by declaring the highest object of knowledge and the sole entirely worthy object of devotion, both in one. He spoke of God's initial and His perpetual relation to the world of nature and to man; holding Him forth as the original Maker who continues to give life and breath to all things by which life and breath are sustained; the original Disposer of the many races of the one family of men in space and time according to the various faces of the earth, that so each might after some special manner seek the God who is not far from those who seek Him after any manner, seeing we are alive to Him, living in Him, not merely receivers of a separate and neutral life. But as He made that original disposition of long continued and widely spread diversity, so now, overlooking those times of necessary ignorance, He was delivering, Paul taught, one common message to mankind, that all everywhere repent, change the direction of their mind; as He in like manner had fixed beforehand a day in which He was about to judge the world in righteousness, that righteousness after which once upon a time so many had toiled and enquired; and this in the person of a man whom He had signified by a token wherein He provided assurance for all men, by raising Him from the dead.

The outcry which ensued broke off the discourse; but the substance was already spoken. In reaching the Resurrection, St Paul had reached the turning point for the restoration of knowledge and of de-

votion. No further progress in knowledge of truth,
beyond what had been already gained and lost, was
possible till that contradiction of average sensible
experience was freely admitted. What had been rough-
ly explored already might be explored afresh in all
imaginable detail, and with new refinements of accu-
racy. But the results would only reaffirm the im-
potence of man to justify to reason his entrance
into the higher levels of truth to which he feels himself invited, so long as he refuses to acknowledge
the light which comes direct from heaven, and
believes that his life is bounded by the range of
his bodily senses. Nor again was any restoration
of healthful devotion possible except by belief in
the God whose will is defined as a will to give life,
and whose power is defined by His giving back life
where death has gone before. Let but that truth,
the truth of God in Christ Jesus, once be firmly
grasped as truth, an endless future was opened for
all knowledge and all devotion.

Wise in the execution of his stewardship, St Paul
in his epistles kept back or put forward his own
cherished contemplation of the Gospel as the perfect
truth according to the state of those to whom he
wrote. His contrast between the milk for babes and
the wisdom which he speaks to them of full age is
indispensable to the understanding of his writings.
The epistles written to churches far advanced in
Christian progress, so that he could venture to name

to them the fulfilment of all things in Christ, are
those which most distinctly bear witness to the deliberate method of his teaching.   While he looks
back with satisfaction in his thanksgivings on "the
Gospel" as a received possession of truth, "the word
of the truth," he looks forward with equal eagerness
in his prayers to the multiplication of a spirit of
knowledge and wisdom, as that which would unlock
the as yet undiscovered wealth buried in the Gospel,
and thereby open out ever better and more fruitful
ways of walking worthily of the Lord.

Throughout the empire, as far we know, the
Church was enlarged by the preaching of the word
of the truth as embodied in the story of Jesus of
Nazareth.   As the wide world to which the nations
belonged came more and more within the apostles'
ken, it is evident that for some of them at least
the conception of truth grew wider.   Yet they did
not cleave the less earnestly to the simple creed of
fact.   The short variable summaries soon needed
expansion, and long oral narratives arose, out of
which, in different places and for special needs, our
first three Gospels were mainly framed.   But moreover in due time truth itself was driven to put on
a new form, by the arising of definite error within
the Christian pale.   Truth could no longer be only
cherished and loved and studied: it had to be
jealously guarded against teaching which threatened
to destroy it.   In the epistles which St Paul wrote

to rulers of the Church, commissioned by himself as
he had been commissioned by Christ, the necessary
change of attitude is conspicuous : while the earlier
language is repeated in all its primitive force, it becomes intermingled with phrases which shew that a
need of sharper definition has arisen.

But it is only in the latest period of the apostolic
age that both the positive and the negative aspects of
truth attain their full proportions. The swaddling
bands of the old Law had been burnt up for ever in
the flames that consumed Jerusalem, and the Church
was entering on the independent course which had
been prefigured in St Paul's position at Rome; it
lived on condition of being Catholic and Ecumenical.
Yet it was threatened by the gravest of dangers from
within : the invasions of falsehood had begun to
banish from belief the primary truths on which alone
a Christian faith could permanently rest.

St John's epistles shew the issue in its true light.
He had to contend with nominal Christians who
strove to disengage an imaginary Christ from the
flesh and blood of the historical Gospel, and in their
practice professed in virtue of their knowledge to be
above morality. But he refuses to deal with knowledge as if it had some independent existence apart
from an object. To him knowledge means access to
truth; and it is the truth known that gives all its
value to knowledge. Hence he resists the movement
which made its boast in knowledge not by disparaging

knowledge but by laying stress on truth, and on the
foundation of truth which the Church had received
from Christ's witnesses. Moreover he seeks to deliver
truth from the unreality of abstraction by recalling
men's eyes to the living Son of God. For knowledge
itself never develops the better part of its own faculties except when it has for its object a living and
free being, one such as we call a person. And on
the other hand such beings are the worthiest objects
of knowledge, affording the best examples of what
known truth means ; and the higher the person, the
higher is the truth and the knowledge of it. Thus,
according to St John's teaching, truth is not perfectly
known except in the knowledge of Him whose name
is the True : such truth alone can entirely fulfil the
office assigned to truth in the life of men, and secure
to other truth its appropriate use.

It is therefore no accident that St John concludes
his chief epistle by saying, "We know that the Son of
God is come, and hath given us an understanding
that we may take knowledge of Him that is true,—
and we are in Him that is true,—in His Son Jesus
Christ" ; so that we now possess both the truth itself
and the faculty and communion for interpreting it :
"this", the God known in His Son Jesus Christ and
lived in in His Son Jesus Christ, "is the true God
and life eternal." To the same purpose again is the
last warning " Little children, keep yourselves from
idols," from gods, that is, that are not true but phan-

toms. For the implicit teaching of the whole New
Testament respecting idols was now brought into clear
light by the effort to create a Christian faith which
should need no foundation in truth. They are not
merely usurping deities, carrying away the homage
due to God alone, but false deities, unrealities that
are not deities at all. The claim of the Father of
the Lord Jesus Christ against them is not simply
that He is the rightful or legitimate, or even the
efficacious God, but that He is the true God.

But this rise of a self-poised knowledge, floating
away from truth, was also a sign to St John that the
time was come when the Gospel itself must be presented more clearly as a declaration of truth than the
earlier needs of the Church had required. There
were words treasured in his memory of which till
then he might have fitly said to the Church, "I have
many things to say to you, but ye cannot carry them
now." These words had to be committed to writing
before he died, and to be adjusted in their right
relation to the words and deeds already familiar to
all. When deceivers set up falsehoods concerning
Christ, it was necessary to insist on truths concerning
Christ. But he would have been leading the Church
into hardly less danger had he allowed its members
to identify any truth, any true doctrine as we say,
concerning Christ with the fontal truth itself which
was given in Him, and of which he was one of the
original witnesses. Lest this danger should arise, even

the truth itself in this its highest power must find a
wider expression, and be called the Light. A man
sent from God could bear witness to the Light: the
Light itself he could never be. But St John had
come to see what was implied in the sum total of
things written in his book and other books concerning Jesus of Nazareth: Jesus was the Truth of
God and the Truth of the Creation by reason of His
own primal relations to both. He was the Word become flesh, even the Word who was in the beginning,
and who was with GOD, and was God. Again,
through Him all things came into being. He was
the Life in which all created life subsisted; and
being the Life of all created things, He was moreover the Light of men, creatures whose prerogative
it was to apprehend the light and know the truth.

This in brief outline is St John's exposition of
Jesus the Christ as the Truth. As his story of the
Gospel alone gives full sense and consistency to the
three other stories of the Gospel, so in these few lines
of the purest and simplest imagery he states, as far
as human language will permit, the truths which
alone give full sense and consistency to his story of
the Gospel. Here were some of the things which
Christ forbore to speak to the Eleven in the days
of His flesh, but into which the Spirit of the Truth,
taking of that which was His, had now conducted
the last of His apostles. Hereby the full measure
of essential truth was at length placed on record for

the Church of after ages.   The secondary revelation
through the apostolic experience was complete.

The generations that followed the writing of the
last Gospel were fertile in dreams of phantasy in
which vast theories of the universe clothed themselves in mythological shapes plucked from incon-
gruous paganisms as well as from the Jewish and
Christian Scriptures.   Some give signs of a profound
ethical or spiritual seriousness.   Nearly all are per-
vaded with an instinct that the redemption in Christ
is in some way the meeting-point for every age and
every world.   Yet the soaring 'knowledge' which
they claim scorns any fixed base of truth.   The old
heathen discords remain unresolved.   The light newly
come into the world has only made the darkness
more visible.

The belief that the Gospel is a message not merely
of salvation but of truth, touching and blessing and
vivifying all other truth, has rarely been wholly
absent except in the worst times.   At two periods in
particular, the most creative since the days of the
apostles, it has come forth with unusual power, and
left results which cannot perish.   In the early days
of the Alexandrian Church it was associated with
a singularly devout and penetrative if also fanciful
study of Scripture.   In the Church of the middle
ages it was associated with the most consistent and
hopeful attempt ever made to set up Christian faith

as the ruling principle in all departments of human
activity. Both attempts were one-sided in different
ways. In the one case the constituents of surrounding society were too corrupt to become themselves
quickened with a new life, and so the chief domain
of truth remained unoccupied; while the leaders of
the Church were by no means free from a spurious
and negative spiritualism, not of Christian but of
secondary heathen origin. In the other, notwith-
standing the freedom and vigour of speculation, the
fixed standard of truth was found less in the original
record itself than in an intermediate tradition, in
which but a part of the pure truth was represented,
and that chiefly as selected and shaped by limited
controversies. In both cases one other fatal hind-
rance intervened. In the new world of Christendom
no truth except theological truth was clearly ascertained; and as theological truth comes easily to be
regarded solely in the light of its obvious religious
uses, truth itself remained a vague and unrealised
conception.

The five centuries of the modern period, diversified
as they have been by inward as well as outward
vicissitude, display one unchanging characteristic in
their results to theology and its relations to knowledge. They have brought successively into cultivation many departments of knowledge, with increasing
pursuit and attainment of truth, and also with increasing relaxation of dependence on theology. The dis-

paragement and isolation of theology has seemed to
go hand in hand with the clear appreciation of truth.
It cannot be denied that in the region of knowledge
as elsewhere there is a possible rivalry between God
and His creatures; and that in the first instance the
homage paid to them is often subtracted from the
homage paid to Him.   But if the Christian faith be
true, His seeming loss is only the condition of greater
gains to come; and it is not hard to discern by what
ways He is even now preparing for Himself a more
perfect sovereignty in the world of known truth.   If
it was the lack of independent standards of truth
which marred the work of theology in former ages,
it is matter for thankfulness that they are no longer
lacking.   Theology is feeble when it attaches itself
by preference to some other base than truth, or
when 'truth' becomes to it no more than the current name for matter of belief received only, not received that it may be known.   But every kind of
truth which is valued and known is a pledge of the
place which truth must hereafter hold in the estima-
tion of the Church, and of the multiplication of all its
energies which the Church will thereby receive.   If
the increasing fear of confounding truth with illusion
tends to discredit that obstinate mental disease by
which the pursuit of truth takes the form of a wandering self-borne 'knowledge' which is not a knowledge of
truth, the result can be only favourable to a faith
of the apostolic type, a faith which finds the primary

truth in One known through a permanent history of words and acts, and learns to understand and employ the truth thus found through a varied and growing experience.

Nor is the character of truth changed by the form in which it is originally acquired: it is no merely verbal bond which unites truth of revelation to truth of discovery. Whether God might be expected to bestow, and whether as a matter of fact He has bestowed, a truth beyond discovery, are legitimate enquiries; though all consistent Christian faith implies the answer. But neither these enquiries, nor any attempts to determine the limits of a revelation, can alter the relations of discovered and revealed truth, supposing both to exist. Truth of discovery is received by every one except the discoverer as much from without as if it were revealed. Truth of revelation remains inert till it has been appropriated by a human working of recognition which it is hard to distinguish from that of discovery. Its initial authority is the first step in a commendation of itself to the conscience and reason, if not of each and at once, yet of many and part by part; in which experience of what lies within the domain of experience becomes in turn the legitimate assurance of what lies above experience.

Once more, theological truth is not divided from other truth by the inscrutable nature of its subject matter. If the revealed knowledge of God receives its form from the limits and peculiarities of human faculty, yet no kind of human knowledge is exempt from the same condition. Theological reflexion does but disturb the habitual unconsciousness which deludes us as to what is involved in the apprehension of any object whatever by finite beings. In like manner the special contradictions which are found to beset all thought on things Divine have their counterparts in every province of knowledge, the moment we lift our eyes from the ground which surrounds our own feet to look into the vanishing distance before and behind. The truth of God revealed in Christ calls not for the separate exercise of an unique faculty, but for the co-operation of every power by which we can read ourselves, and hold converse with whatever is not ourselves. Christian theology has in it indeed an element which other knowledge has not; but it embraces all elements that are scattered elsewhere.

As the progress in knowledge in the later ages must ultimately invigorate theology by throwing into stronger relief its character as simply truth, so also the new worlds conquered for knowledge give promise to aid powerfully in bringing to light the unity of all truth in Him who said "I am the Truth," and thus in raising knowledge of truth to the place which He marked out for it in the gathering of man to God. The first new world, the world of man himself, was in part the discovery of an old world long buried out of

sight : the revival of the classical past had no small
share in making human life and thought and language the subject of conscious and methodical study.
The second new world, the world of nature, was in
most respects altogether new ; and the rank which it
has vindicated for itself as an object of serious and
lofty knowledge materially changes the view which
must henceforth be taken of knowledge as a whole,
and therefore of its primary structure. But how is
theology affected by the change? Does the knowledge of nature tend, so far as it prevails, to subvert
the old order of things in the midst of which the
Christian revelation took its rise, and with it to
subvert the foundations of what has heretofore appeared to be the knowledge of God? Or is the
knowledge of nature only fulfilling a function designed for it from the first, bringing to light a part
of the revelation in Christ Himself which God in His
wisdom has hidden as it were under a veil till the
fulness of time be come?

An attempt to give a full answer to these questions, among the gravest that can occupy us either
for present necessity or for any forecast of the future, would require the discussion of several familiar
problems which lie beyond our subject, and which cannot be rightly handled in a cursory manner. There
are however considerations, arising out of our own
place in the history of the human appropriation of
truth, which may furnish at least a fitting preparation

for reflexion on these high themes; nay which perhaps carry us nearer to the true central parting of
the ways of belief than do the controversies that
seem in their isolation to raise more definite issues.

Let us then begin by looking around and looking
back.   Man stands between God above and the world
beneath, in intimate relations with each; and even so
stands the knowledge of man.   It is by a true instinct
that man seeks first to know himself; and that, when
in pursuing other knowledge he has been led into
contemplating its objects as alien and distant, he
presently returns eagerly to that which is his own and
is near, and marvels why he wandered from himself.
Yet strive as he may, he cannot know himself while
he knows only himself.   In making the effort, he cannot attain to more than that inchoate wisdom which
precedes knowledge and is incessantly at fault for
want of knowledge.   God and the outer world have
both so large a portion in man himself that in abjuring the knowledge of them he condemns the knowledge of himself to loss and distortion of truth.   In
knowledge as in all else he labours in vain to be
independent: he is most himself when he receives
most, and most freely acknowledges that he receives.
But the lesson is toilsome to learn, and it cannot
be learned all at once.   It has been God's will that
man should learn first the one part of it, and then the
other.

In the Christian revelation, as we have already

seen, the knowledge of truth was for the first time set
in its proper place as necessary to sound life and
rightful action. But further its own proper subject
was the knowledge of God, and this was the knowledge which it set before mankind to be learned first.
The whole range of truth contained in Christ was, so
to speak, opened from above: the first truth disclosed
in Him was the truth of God. This truth alone was
essential to the most indispensable of the gifts given
in Christ, the life of the spirit in faith, hope, and love,
and thus to the constraining of all lower things into
the service of life. As the fear of God is the beginning of all wisdom, so the knowledge of God is
the surest entrance into all knowledge. Through the
primacy of theology all the parts of knowledge are
best maintained in their true place, and knowledge
itself holds its true place amidst that which is not
knowledge.

Hereby was marked out the office of the ancient
Church. In labouring to appropriate for its own
needs the original Gospel of truth under the guidance
of the Spirit of the truth, it wrought out a Christian
theology. It was doubtless inevitable that imperfections should accompany the work. Men engrossed
with cultivating the knowledge of God, and seeing
around them little that was not vile where the knowledge of God was absent, might easily come to speak
as though no other truth or knowledge of truth were
needful or even salutary for men. From this and

other historical causes, the work itself could hardly be final within its own limits, much less complete. Moreover insuperable limitations were inherent in the nature of the task; for all communicable knowledge is but as the skeleton of the total knowledge. Yet it is through the communicable part of knowledge that the perception of one man is in any measure imparted to many, or of one generation to succeeding generations. The Christian life cannot dispense with separate derivative Christian truths, though Christ alone is the Truth. In the unfolding and ascertainment of theological doctrine various ages have their tasks to perform, according to their several opportunities: but the thoughts of the earliest ages exercise in all after times a sway which it would be equally futile and mischievous to gainsay. Their work was done to good effect for many centuries; and the services which it has rendered and assuredly has still to render will never be appreciated till it is itself truthfully and intelligently known.

But if it was necessary that man should come to know God above, it was also necessary that he should come to know the world below. The elder knowledge was itself imperfect, and always tending to become the shadow of a once substantial knowledge, so long as the younger was unborn; and it failed at last to maintain that power over life and action without which the conventional honour which it received was vain. It is well for other purposes than the satisfaction of curiosity, or the enlargement of material utility that the earth and its inhabitants in all grades of being, and the worlds of space around it, are in these later centuries increasingly known; and that to these effective reforms and extensions of crude ancient knowledge are now yet later added a knowledge of the constituent elements and forces of the world, and of its history in the past.

The legitimate influence of so vast a body of more or less ascertained truth comes near to us in several ways. It is truth concerning a variety of deeply interesting objects presented incessantly to our senses, and rousing our senses from base to noble use. It is truth concerning a multitude of beings by means of which we ourselves live, and by the presence of which our lives are incessantly affected. Yet more, it is truth converging upon our own bodies, true parts of ourselves, yet sharers in countless structures and forces of every grade beneath us. Whether we were moulded out of the dust of the earth immediately or through an ascending series of lower beings, the world of nature can no longer be an alien world. On the strength of the knowledge already securely won, setting aside all disputed and disputable problems, we must henceforth as men feel a true kinship to the earth and to all that lives upon it.

Whatever other effects this advancing knowledge may have on the thoughts and ways of men in after days, one effect at least is already manifest. As it is chiefly the knowledge of the lower world which has been instrumental in making the idea of truth vivid and mighty, so men's thoughts of truth in general have come to be mainly determined by this single region of truth. It follows that we are tempted to judge of ourselves and all that is above us by measures and procedures taken exclusively from things below us. This view of the universe cannot but strive more and more to become complete, coherent, and exclusive. If once we fully accept the authority of the earth to give the law to all our thoughts, we cannot rest satisfied with a truth limited to the earth. The short-comings of actual knowledge must be eked out by soaring imaginations calling themselves knowledge, as of old, but borrowing from ascertained truth no more than suggestions; while an inward necessity drives them to exclude God from the domain of knowledge, and to depict all in man that seeks God or answers to His seeking as exceptional disease.

For, as we stand between things above and things below, and our knowledge like our nature partakes of both, the truth which we recognise must lead us either upwards or downwards. It has always been hard for man to stand erect while discarding the truth of God sent down from heaven. It was hard of old, while he seemed to himself to be an independent being, severed by an impassable chasm from all lower things, and therefore able to pursue a separate perfection. But now, as the chasm closes, and the earth's full force is permitted to act on man, it becomes impossible for him to lift up his head in his ancient dignity unless there be a countervailing force from on high. No god-like thoughts or feelings within, no conjectured or fabricated divinities without, can restore him to himself, much less raise him to the better self towards which he fain would still aspire. When once he has learned to know truth, he cannot be permanently sustained by any power which is separate from truth. Nothing less will avail than the true God in the heavens, truly known, as He is known to His Church in His Son Jesus Christ our Lord. If the children of God find it a hard struggle to resist the fostering earth when she draws them down in the might of her own partial truth, yet He who said " I am the Truth" said also " I if I be lifted up out of the earth will draw all men unto Myself."

On the other hand we may well believe that an office of unmixed good is likewise reserved for the knowledge of the lower world. It is not too much to say that the Gospel itself can never be fully known till nature as well as man is fully known ; and that the manifestation of nature as well as man in Christ is part of His manifestation of God. As the Gospel is the perfect introduction to all truth, so on the other hand it is itself known only in proportion as it is used for the enlightenment of departments of truth which seem at first sight to lie beyond its boundaries. It remains true, as of old, that no adequate revelation

of God to man could take place except in the Son of
man : the divinity whom man supposes himself to
behold when he confines his gaze to the lower world
is no true God.   But when once the primary human
revelation has been given and recognised, then all
lower forms can bear their part to make up the
fulness of truth, such truth as is accessible to man.
Man detached from the world is not the man whom
fact and revelation make known.   A Son of man
detached from the world would not be the Son of
man of the Gospel; he would not be the Word
without whom nothing came into being, or the Life
of all things living.   To deny the redemption of the
body is to deny Christ and relapse into heathen
despair ; and the redemption of the body carries with
it the redemption of the world to which it belongs.

As we can seldom bathe ourselves in the freshness
of living things without coming forth with purified
and brightened hearts, even such let us believe may
be the effect of the truth of nature on our thoughts of
God Himself.   The substance of our faith in Him
can come only from that one Life and Death and
Resurrection into the fellowship of which we as men
are permitted to enter ; and the primary lore through
which our faith is deepened and enlarged is always
the human lore, the knowledge of what men have
done and thought and felt, and above all of their
words, the most comprehensive treasure-house of their
experience.   But the earth as well as the heaven is

full of God's glory, and His visible glory is but the garment of His truth; so that every addition to truth becomes a fresh opportunity for adoration.

Thus the strictest sense of Christ's words "I am the Truth" is also the most comprehensive: it answers alike to the requirements of the hour when it was spoken, and to the gradual fulfilment of the Divine kingdom. It points first to that manifestation of the unseen God of which He spoke when He said "He that hath seen me hath seen the Father"; while it includes in its ultimate scope all creation, the world of nature of which He is the Life, and the world of man whom He redeemed out of nature, and of whom He is both the Life and the Light. This second declaration like the first spoke comfort and hope to the faint-hearted disciples by disclosing to them the depth and range of the Lord's own permanent working, and therefore of the work which they were to carry forward in His name. It speaks comfort and hope in like manner to all at any time who find themselves perplexed by the presence of truth not before known. It warns of the danger of suffering truth to lose its rightful place in work and devotion. It marks every truth which seems alien to Christ as a sign that the time is come for a better knowledge of Christ, since no truth can be alien to Him who is the Truth. It points to Him in His eternal fulness as the one sufficient measure by which all truth may find its proper station. The comfort and hope thus bestowed

by Christ were dependent on the demand which He
made.   If it was an arduous change after following
the Lord as a Guide to walk in Him as the universal
Way, it could not be less arduous to pass from
hearkening to Him as a Teacher to studying Him as
the universal Truth.   The duly rendered service of
any truth is stern discipline: what then must the
service be of Him who is the Truth of truths?

Accordingly the burden then laid on the Eleven
becomes an image of the burden laid on the Church
now.   There has perhaps never been a time when the
Church has been absolutely content with accepting
the body of inherited doctrine without any attempts,
conscious or unconscious, to verify its truth in one
mode or another.   But still, through the many centuries since the need of security against plausible
error compelled the Church to press into the moulds
of the human understanding that which can never be
so pressed without some loss or even distortion, tradition, at certain periods corrected by an appeal to
Scripture or some intermediate authority, has on the
whole been accepted as a sufficient guarantee of truth.
If now, by a voice which cannot be disobeyed, the
Church is summoned to know as truth what it has
hitherto chiefly held as sacred tradition, the prospect
may seem as alarming as when the disciples learned
that the Teacher's voice would soon be no longer
heard among them.   We might well be alarmed if we

could believe that either the former supremacy of authoritative tradition or its impending decline were without a purpose in the counsels of God. Perhaps we are none of us yet in a position to estimate rightly how much we have owed to that long-continued externality in the form of truth which there is a strong temptation to condemn as inherently vicious. But thus much at least we can see, that it has enabled the Church to be nourished by its inherited store from age to age, while it was engaged in other tasks not less necessary for its active work in the world; and that it has deferred this more difficult task of ascertaining the full value of the inheritance till the maturity procured by that long and varied education.

Nor must it be supposed that tradition and authority can ever become useless in matters of truth. In any state of things which we can at present conceive, a large proportion of the members of the Church must still for the fundamentals of their belief be in a state of partial tutelage. Nay, perhaps those who are themselves best exercised in unwearied and courageous search will be the readiest to profess how much they have been helped throughout towards clear and dispassionate vision by the gracious pressure of some legitimate tradition or other authority, into the limits of whose jurisdiction they had seldom occasion to enquire.

But the call to the study of the Church's heritage of truth as truth proceeds also from the call to a

new field of labour. The later stage of discipleship
is an apostleship. Hitherto the Church has been
mainly feeding for itself on the truth which it possessed. Now it must learn to go forth beyond its
own borders and put its truth to fresh uses. As the
Apostles went forth to reduce all the nations without
to discipleship, so now it is ours to carry that light
which alone is the light of life into all the outlying
worlds of knowledge as of action and of life. If
'because of the time we ought to be teachers', surely
'by reason of use' we must now 'have our powers
of sense exercised toward discernment of good and
evil', and be able to bear 'the strong meat' of truth,
the 'word' or doctrine or reason 'of righteousness'.

The enterprise is full of peril; yet its peril is but
the inverted image of its promise. If we accept the
command to 'prove all things', and 'hold fast that
which is good', we must be prepared for the possibility
of having to cast aside at last, after the most patient
and watchful trial, this or that which we have been
accustomed to receive as true. How far the loss if
it comes will be other than a semblance of loss, or
how far it will be outweighed by unlooked-for gains,
we may not know. Assuredly many will take part
in the trial unversed in all the needful discipline,
enslaved to inappropriate modes of investigation,
ignorant of what patience and watchfulness mean,
reckless meanwhile in inflicting wanton injury on all
forms of human welfare except the one or two which

circumstances have enabled them to appreciate. Assuredly many a weak or hasty soul will be stricken with spiritual palsy, and many a strong soul with sadness, while the work goes on. Yet so it has been in every great crisis of the Church by which the kingdom of God has made a swift advance. If we stop to count the falling or fallen, no battle will ever be won.

But do we fear for the fate of the costly truth itself? It may be reasonable that we should fear, if we have never known it in our inmost hearts, shining upon us with a vividness that makes the clearness of common truths seem like a pallid mist. If we have, we surely cannot believe that any multiplication of trials can ever extinguish its central light. Or is it that we fear so greatly the folly and feebleness of human judgement, that we think the truth may be driven by processes of frenzied ignorance from the belief and acceptance of man? Yes if it be not truth indeed, and the truth of God ; and if Christ came not into the world to bear witness to the truth. This at least let us who have been taught by the Gospel believe, that no faith founded on truth can ever die except that it may rise to a better life. Believed or not believed, known or not known, it abides for ever in heaven till the hour appointed by the Father. In so far as we have hitherto been content not to know Him whom we have believed, let us thankfully learn to know Him better now, for

so only shall we be persuaded that He is able to
guard that which He has committed to our charge,
and committed it for stewardship and distribution,
and not for hoard.

But as the relaxation in the stress exerted by traditional authority is an occasion of troubling to the
Church as a body, so to those whose eyes are now
first opening to the bright world of knowledge it is an
occasion of exulting joy. The past of parental teaching, or the past of an authoritative creed, is looked
back upon as a bondage in the midst of the air of
freedom which seems to waft truth gaily in upon the
soul with every wandering breath. Truth, perfect
truth, seems always close at hand, excluded by nothing save the restraints which men have forged for
sight and thought. We, who have learned how much
delusion there is in these brilliant dreams, ought never
to forget the power of blessing, nay, the truth, that is
in them. They are true as to the end, false only as
to the means by which the end can and must be
reached. Bonds exist that men may be free ; traditions exist that men may see and know: but it is very
hard for one and all of us to keep our eyes steadily
fixed on these fundamental truths in their integrity.
Meanwhile the unfaltering faith in truth is, next to
the faith in Christ crucified and risen, perhaps the
power in man on which the future of human welfare
most depends, certainly that which in this place most

deserves to be cherished as a holy fire. It is quenched only too easily in after years by a thousand elements of seeming experience without and within, good as well as evil. It dies out in many who once were inspired by it, choked by coarse interests, or suppressed for the sake of some other spirit which it is fondly supposed must reign alone. Whatever therefore gives it energy and endurance is good ; and the time when it springs up is a time to rejoice in.

Yet that its promise may be fulfilled, there are delusions to be unlearned. The subjection to early teaching was or should have been no bondage at all, but the one indispensable condition of a strong and timely growth. Without the regimen of a fixed and prescribed form of truth the faculties run riot in premature licence, and gain nothing but disablement for effective operation hereafter. Nor is the influence of a tempered authority in matters of truth less salutary after the first or second probation is over. The air is thick with bastard traditions which carry us captive unawares while we seem to ourselves to be exercising our freedom and our instinct for truth. The traditions of the hour or the age are as indubitably external to us, and as little founded of necessity on freshly perceived truth, as any traditions of the past. The danger of them lies in their disguise. The single negative fact that they make war on some confessed tradition prevents us from discovering that they too draw their force no less from an authority, until it is too late and we have lost or damaged that power of independent vision which is but braced and harmonised by a known and honoured tradition.

The perception of truth depends as much on the state of him that desires to perceive as on the objects that are presented to his view. No slight or swift or uniform process will enable any one to master the mere art of discerning truth from false appearance. But, not to speak of this most needful and most various mental preparation, there is another condition which is never forgotten with impunity. The more we know of truth, the more we come to see how manifold is the operation by which we take hold of it. It is not reached through one organ but through many. No single faculty, if indeed there be any single faculties, can arrogate a right to exclude from the domain of truth what cannot be readily subjected to its own special action. It may be that no element of our compound nature is entirely shut out from taking part in knowledge. It is at all events certain that the specially mental powers will never be able to judge together in rightful relation when the nature as a whole is disordered by moral corruption. There is no evil passion cherished, no evil practice followed, which does not cloud or distort our vision whenever we look beyond the merest abstract forms of things. There is a truth within us, to use the language of Scripture, a perfect inward ordering as of a transparent crystal, by which alone the faithful image of truth without us is brought within our ken. Not in vain said the Lord that it is the pure in heart, they whose nature has been subdued from distraction into singleness, who shall see God ; or, we may add, who shall see the steps of the ladder by which we may mount to God.

The stedfast and prescient pursuit of truth is therefore itself a moral and spiritual discipline. We cannot render it perfect service without walking in the way which is Christ, and living in the life which is Christ. Every flaw and scar of our nature will go to mar the image of truth which we can attain to. Even if it were not so, yet to know in part is a fixed condition of our life here. There will always be spots and clouds of darkness, difficulties as we call them, in the midst of even our brightest light. The knowledge which again and again yields fresh sustenance to faith is not ordained to displace faith as the moving power of our lives.

The pursuit of truth begins in a sense of freedom. We almost make truth itself the symbol of freedom for the workings of our minds. We are slow to learn that truth is never that which we choose to believe, but always that which we are under a necessity to believe. In proportion to the earnestness of the pursuit we discover that we must needs be servants where we thought to be masters. A life devoted to truth is a life of vanities abased and ambitions forsworn. We have to advance far in the willing servitude before we recognise that it is creating for us a new and another freedom. The early dream was not false : only freedom comes last, not first. The order of experience corresponds with the order of the Lord's promises which He offered to those who had begun to believe Him : " If ye abide in my word, ye are truly disciples of mine, and " then " ye shall know the truth, and" then " the truth shall make you free."

LECTURE III

I AM ... THE LIFE.

THE better heathenisms at their height were
religions of life. This was the source of their greatest power. The chief causes of their fall proceeded
from the inevitable limitations of that life which
alone they were able to express and uphold. It was
divided into many separate and exclusive lives. It
was a fluctuating and transitory life, dependent solely
on the human emotions which it should have sustained, and therefore itself subject to the same en-
croachments from without and from below which
struck them sick and killed them. It was a life
confined within the sphere of emotion, and therefore
incapable of progress. It was divided from knowledge, and therefore knowledge was able to bear a
part in destroying it. Its chief influence over action
was by way of restraint. It was a life which sought
satisfaction within the confines of the present, and so
could often dispense with hope, though it could not
annihilate fear. But these limitations do not set

aside the fact that life itself was once the glory of heathenism.

In time the heathen world for the most part ceased to possess life, or to care for it. The sense of life had always been accompanied by pleasure and now, for nearly all, it was only pleasure that remained behind in the vacant place of life. Death, which it had once been possible to hide or forget in the strength of life, refused to be hidden or forgotten any longer. The presence of the threatening spectre might at last be felt as a zest to pleasure; but as against the remnants of the antecedent life it was omnipotent. Nor was life abandoned only by the thoughtless. The depression or abnegation of life became the refuge of the wise and the good. Life, they knew, made men vulnerable in proportion to its variety and intensity. Whether their desire was to ward off misery and maintain serenity, or to avoid wickedness and cherish virtue, in either case it was prudent not to feel overmuch, for so opportunity would be offered to the enemy. The individual soul and body together, or the individual soul fortified against its body as the nearest camp of the enemy, could maintain independence only by a lowering of life, a tempering of life with death.

Knowledge had grown, or seemed to grow, after life had begun to sink: but as life sank more and mo e, knowledge at length failed also. The cause of failure lay not merely in the intrinsic difficulty of the

problems attempted, or the inadequacy of the means
then within reach for solving them, but in the drying
up of the impulse to seek truth, and even of the capacity for recognising it. For no sense that knowledge
is wanted for practical necessities, much more no restlessness of neutral curiosity, can give resolution or
consistent clearness to enquiry, if the stream of life
itself be languid. Enquiry is but a figure of speech
for men enquiring: and men cannot long enquire to
any purpose concerning any great subject when they
have sunk to welcoming death within themselves as
an ally and friend.

Israel also had a full share of the natural and
spontaneous life of antiquity. It lasted long, and
it revived once and again after times of decline. But
the life of Israel was lived in the presence of the
Lord God: it was always subordinate to obedience
and faith towards One above. He was always known
as walking among the trees of man's garden, a joy
and glory to the worshipper, a terror to the trans-
gressor. His government abounded in disciplinary
restraints on life, while it never favoured the suppression of life, or its dishonour. Nor was the providential teaching without lasting results in the people.
Israel alone held fast an ancient integrity of nature,
neither tolerating, much less glorifying moral corruption on the one hand, nor seeking freedom from evil
or nearness to God in the stunting or frustration of
life on the other.

The sense of life which Israel enjoyed was however best expressed in the choice of the name ' life '
as a designation of that higher communion with God
which grew forth in due time as the fruit of obedience
and faith. The psalmist or wise man or prophet,
whose heart had sought the face of the Lord, was
conscious of a second or divine life of which the first
or natural life was at once the image and the foundation ; a life not imprisoned in some secret recess of
his soul, but filling his whole self, and overflowing
upon the earth around him. It did not estrange him
from the natural life which he shared with other men
or with lower creatures, and which he was taught to
regard as proceeding from God's own breath or spirit.
But it withheld him from seeking satisfaction within
the lower life alone : and it made itself known not as
a Divinely ordained substitute for life, for the sake of
which life must be foregone ; but as itself a life indeed,
the crown of all life.

There is no life, worthy to be called life, entirely
separate from joy and gladness. The lower life
when it exists in any strength, has in it at once a
gladness of personal energy and a delight in the
gladness of all living creatures as it is displayed in
their youth or comeliness. The higher life for Israel
could never be wanting in this characteristic. It was
essentially a joy in the Lord ; not an acquiescence in
His counsels but a sympathy with them. It was partial indeed, and sometimes feeble and perplexed, as

the sympathy of dwellers on the earth with the Most
High. It took the form of response; it was a turning
back to Him on His seeking. But this recognition
of its derivative nature did but lift it the higher
above the perils of earthly vicissitude, and bring a
wider circle of earthly existence within its scope.

"With Thee", says the Psalmist, "is the fountain
of life". The perennial spring of water that leaps
and flashes as though it were a living thing, breaking
ceaselessly forth from a hidden source, is the best
image of that higher life bestowed on him to whom
God has unveiled His face. Other things that have
a brilliant life grow sick and waste and die: but the
fountain's life leaps on from generation to generation.
Such, the Israelite felt, is the life which man can find
provided for him in God. The spontaneous uncultured joy of spring or of youth is short lived. It
dies out with the mere lapse of time. In men it is
liable to be prematurely choked with labours and
cares. But he whose heart has learned to make
answer to the Lord comes to find that the power of
life and joy lives on with him while outward things
are taking their course of obstruction or decay. He
has a life exempt from being dried up, for it flows
not from within himself or from any part of the
perishable creation but from an ever living fountain
in the heavens.

But in the later days before Christ came the
honour of life as the supreme good was wellnigh lost

7—2

in Israel.   Life in the lower sense had come to mean
little more than existence, the bare continuance and
working of soul and body through a term of years.
Life in the higher sense had come to mean only a
future existence; bright in contrast with the present,
but seldom with the brightness of life, and not to be
entered without the extinction of the present life.
Lofty thoughts were not wanting about the blessing
that accompanies fear of God and trust in Him.
Wisdom in particular as a Divine gift was celebrated
not unworthily with exalted praises.   It was no
grovelling or trivial form of wisdom that was thus
extolled, but one by which 'friends of God and
prophets' are created; a wisdom in which God was
the Guide, Himself 'the corrector of the wise'.   Yet
language spoke no more of life in the old high sense;
and the silence was a true token of the loss which
had been suffered in thought and feeling.   Every high
aspiration, whether it was a hope of a future existence, or a hope of a coming deliverer, or a pursuit
of deep things known only to the sage, was a flight
into a distant region.   In no sense was life itself an
acknowledged link either with the world below or
with God above.

Whatever life had anywhere been found and lost,
whatever life had never been found, was given to man
in Christ.   It may be that this or that portion of the
vast inheritance of life has never as yet been claimed,

or has been but doubtfully claimed, because faith in Him has been too petty or wilful in its scope as well as too feeble in its energy. But in Christ life was given in its fulness nevertheless, and in that due subordination which alone secures that nothing be lost. This is the one character of the Gospel which takes precedence of all others: its many partial messages are unfoldings of its primary message of life. Salvation according to Scripture is nothing less than the preservation, restoration or exaltation of life: while nothing that partakes or can partake of life is excluded from its scope; and as is the measure, grade, and perfection of life, such is the measure, grade, and perfection of salvation.

This the true nature of Christ's work, as the restoration of life in the most comprehensive sense, is conspicuously shown from the beginning by the contrast with John the Baptist which all the Gospels exhibit. The austerity of John himself, and the stern rigour with which he preached purification and separation in his war against the evil deeds of Israel, might regarded alone have seemed to mark him as only reviving a departed time, and making no new step in the history of God's people. But this work of his was clearly signified by himself to be a well-considered preparation for One whose office should be different and entirely new. In John the law of Moses spoke out once more at its highest force as a law, uttered in the language and depicted in the

symbolic acts of an early prophet. At the dawning
presence of Him who was coming all the partial
anticipations of His work disappeared. The vague
evangelic hopes of the later prophets were kept back.
In their place were given the positive assertions
relating to the present and the immediate future :
" The kingdom of heaven hath drawn nigh ": " there
cometh he that is stronger than I after me, of whom
I am not meet to stoop and loose the latchet of his
shoes." The old mountain-thunder of Sinai for the
last time uttered its voice in John, that the voice of
the Son of man might be heard in tones of clearer
truth.

The stronger than John the Baptist was named
Saviour from His mother's womb, and His saving
was part of His lordship. He came as the Anointed
King's Son to His own inheritance, to deliver a holy
land and a holy people from invaders and usurpers,
and to bind up the breaches and severances which
they had wrought. Sometimes the intruders are
diseases or disablements, sometimes they are sins,
sometimes they are unclean spirits in whose working
disease and sin are inextricably blended. But in all
cases the expulsion is called an act of saving or
salvation ; and it follows on that homage to the
rightful Sovereign above, and to Him whom He has
sent, which is called faith.

And so always the precious possession which is
rescued out of the hand of the enemies is Life. That

one name alone expresses the summed result of Christ's acts of various and limited salvation. The diseases, weaknesses, cripplings, losses of sight or speech or hearing, and losses of the governing reason, whether they had but lately come to pass or were of long standing or existed from birth, were only so many inroads of death, partial assimilations of the living body to the inert mimicry of the corpse. The healings and restorations were but differing gifts of life that had been lost, renewals of some one of those forms or activities or faculties of the united body and soul which make up the single picture of life. Even the restoration of a withered hand is spoken of as a part of what is emphatically called 'saving a soul' as opposed to 'slaying'; of saving, that is, the central and supreme seat of life within the body from the death which in slaying it would slay not one member but all. And conversely the raisings from the dead appear only as undoings of a more complete mastery exercised by death. Concerning the daughter announced to lie dead it is promised that "she shall be saved": the father of the dying boy is told simply " Thy son liveth ".

On the other hand the adversary, the prince of the invading powers, is represented as having his desires faithfully expressed in the will of the murderous Jews. As he was the enemy of truth, so also of life : he was a manslayer from the beginning. And the traitorous disciple, who consents to deliver up his Lord to death, is branded with the same character. "None of the disciples perished save the son of perdition". He who forsook the ministry of salvation and life, and gave himself up to wasting and spoiling and destroying, was by a righteous necessity compelled to waste and spoil and destroy himself. For the ministries of life and of death alike are the same within that they are without.

As Christ expelled the enemies of life, so also He provided for its support. The lower and [seemingly] lifeless parts of creation subsist after a fashion without nourishment: but a living creature depends for the continuance of its life upon what it receives from other creatures, and if the proper nourishment is withheld, every faculty of body and soul languishes and at last dies. It was fitting that the Lord of life should wonderfully bestow not merely life itself but that without which life was in the ordinary course of things impossible: and this He did when He multiplied food that the hungry multitude might be fed. Nor was His action independent of the inferior life which He found before Him : His heavenly aid flowed in earthly channels. He took that which was brought Him, and blessed it, and lo it was multiplied as it came from the disciples' distributing hands. Thus the renewal of life which proceeded from Him was supplied through the medium of the earth's own produce, and conveyed through the medium of men in whom dwelt no independent power.

By signs like these Christ displayed His care for all the lower life of man, and His purpose and power to reach and restore it. But there is another life in which it culminates, a life rooted in that lower life and fed from it, yet soaring above it, the highest flower and fruit of man when God is not as yet known, the life of the various human affections. In the fervour of this life gladness rises into joy, and pain into sorrow. Both alike are manifestations of the life, and exercises of it whereby it is continually quickened. Into both alike Christ entered, and by the felt communion of His presence gave new life to the life within. Now to a father, now to a widowed mother, now to sisters, now to a master, He came nigh in their trouble and sorrow with a threefold salvation, life to the object of their love, life to themselves in the might of His sympathy, and perennial and unbounded life to all in faith in the Father above to whom He lifted up His own eyes.

As He gave food to the lower life as well as expelled its enemies, so also He came not merely as a healer to the life of natural affection in its sorrow but also as the renewer and multiplier of its joy. The first of all His miracles, the act which He made, St John says, as a beginning of His signs, a silent prophecy of His full salvation, took place at a marriage, the highest festival of natural life even when it is nothing more. Doubtless His own presence and guileless fellowship of joy gave much. But more

was to come. The first gift which He gave as the
Son of God was the wine of gladness, poured forth at
the appointed hour from what in its origin was water.
The first or merely natural supply of wine had failed ;
but that which came unseen in its place at its Lord's
command was the same and yet better ; and so the
human joy received promise of enrichment and exaltation from heaven.

By these steps Christ ascended to the height of His
purpose. For above all He restored and more than
restored, the nobler life which Psalmists and other
men of old had found in communion with God. His
lower works [would have been] unmeaning without
this supreme purpose ; while the universal office and
range of the higher Life would never have been felt
had he not shown that all Life came within His
domain as destined to be man's sphere and instrument. But it was only to disciples that He could
impart it, and the progress of their discipleship was
ever leading them more deeply into it. But it was
not an esoteric entrancement, beginning only when
the sights and sounds of daily intercourse were forgotten. Every word of His in public or private,
every action, every look and gesture, was a lesson in
the life. His acts of life-giving in the lower sphere
were the foundation of His life-giving in the higher
sphere. Every thing which entered into earthly life
became the image and the vehicle of a Divine grace,
a spark of the eternal life.

The life thus given was a life in God. It rested on the feeling that the Father in heaven, who once had seemed so distant, had now been brought nigh to those who looked for Him. The sense of this nearness was the highest condition of life. Yet not the less was the life in God dependent on discipleship to Christ. We call it a gift, but it was a gift inseparable from the person of the Giver. It was through trustful communion with the Lord who walked in their midst as one of themselves that they learned the meaning of trustful communion with the Most High; as it was also through participation in His own life of joyful obedience that they came to know how the heavenly will can be done on earth, and the earthly life be quickened in the doing. On the other hand this intimate communion was equally dependent on their growing sense of His authority: in proportion as they felt Him to be their Lord, they were able to feel Him near and to welcome His nearness.

Thus far we have been tracing some of the chief elements of life as we find them in the records of the earlier Evangelists and also, somewhat more distinctly, in narratives by St John in which life itself is not named. But his office of binding together the teachings of his predecessors by bringing to light and to distinct expression the underlying and uniting bases of truth is perfected in his testimony concerning life.

The word is not indeed absent from the first three Gospels, though it is rarer there than we might have expected from its importance in the Old Testament. When a ruler asks how he may obtain an inheritance of 'eternal life,' our Lord accepts from his lips the too trite phrase which, after its first suggestion by the language of the Psalms had been brought into general use by its occurrence in a conspicuous verse of the book of Daniel. But at the same time, partly by the whole tenour of His answers, partly by bringing in the ideas of entrance into the kingdom of God and entrance into the life, He implicitly restores to the phrase a truer sense than that implied in the question, and current in the debased religion of the time.

In this as in other cases St John's Gospel gives distinct verbal expression to what the other Gospels relate but do not name. We have already had occasion to notice the character of the first miracle, significantly marked as the first, which St John records. Twice shortly afterwards he digresses from his narrative to dwell on the purpose of our Lord's coming as being to make faith possible, and on eternal life as being the work and fruit of such faith: and in like manner at the original close of the Gospel he declares himself to have written to the end that his readers might believe that Jesus is the Christ, the Son of God, and that believing they might have life in His name.

In more varied combinations, but not less distinctly, does the name of 'life' run through our Lord's own words as reported by St John. Beside Jacob's well or fountain and at the solemn water-drawing in the Temple He uses the familiar phrase 'living water' in a sense of His own, which had been also the sense of the prophets. When He has fed the hungry multitudes, He calls Himself the Bread of God which descended and giveth life to the world, the very Bread of the Life. In contrast to the destroying thief He proclaims Himself to be the Good Shepherd, come that the sheep may have life, and that they may have overflowing abundance.

While on the one hand He speaks of this life in language drawn from the ordinary life of nature on which it is in a manner founded, on the other He attributes to it a different and more wondrous origin. The first stage of the process of life is within the Godhead: "As the Father hath life in Himself, so also He gave to the Son to have life in Himself." The bestowal on man is but another stage of the same process: "as the living Father sent me, and I live because of the Father, he also that eateth me, even he shall live because of me." And there is a third stage in which men become in their turn subordinate sources of life : " he that believeth on me, as the Scripture said, rivers out of his belly shall flow of living water."

Thus the result of our Lord's varied teaching

about life is to exhibit it as the ultimate and fundamental form of human good, the highest and the
deepest blessing which man can in any wise attain ;
and that especially because it is what most closely
links him to God, and may most truly be represented
as issuing from God's own being. But while the
disciples were being led by this gradual and often
indirect guidance to esteem rightly the preciousness
of life, they were learning also in like manner that
the life thus highly exalted was in some sense embodied in the person of their Lord. After the earlier
days of intercourse had brought them to recognise
Him as a trustworthy teacher concerning life and the
way to attain it, nay as Himself a giver of it, they
soon came to feel that when He was giving them life
He was giving them of Himself, for they received it
after a fashion which the externality of such terms
as 'given' and 'gift' renders them incompetent to
describe.

Life came forth from the Lord to the disciples
through everything in Him which they were able to
apprehend. But the chief agency by which it was
conveyed was His sayings. The life in them was all
the mightier because they were charged with other
contents besides life. Through His sayings He
guided, and through His sayings He taught. They
were lessons in the Way and the Truth, and for that
reason they were able to give articulate expression to
the inarticulate life beneath. It is this quality in our

Lord's sayings that accounts for the frequency with
which He refers to them, and the substantiality with
which He appears sometimes to invest them; now
laying stress on their contents as the 'word' or
declaration of truth, of which they were at once parts
and expressions; now setting them forth simply as
utterances, things spoken and things heard, that is as
effluxes, so to say, from a personal speaker. Here
too the process on earth is represented as having its
beginning in heaven: what things soever the disciples
hear the Lord speak are but repeated from what He
has heard the Father speak. The sayings and the
life alike and together descend upon them through
the Son from the Father.

This intimate connexion between our Lord's sayings and the Divine life communicated to men is
brought into unusual prominence at the close of that
long discourse on the Bread of the Life, which St John
represents as proving a stumbling block to many of
the disciples, and leading to their departure from the
company. Their murmuring was evidently an echo
of the murmurings of the Jews during the discourse:
they could not accept the announced descent of the
Divine bread out of the heaven, so unlike the descent,
invisible though it was itself, of the visible and tangible manna. Our Lord in reply pointed onwards to
a time when the form of the Son of man might be
seen reversing the descent by ascending up on high,
and then exposed the unbelief which ascribed a life-

giving power to visible things, because it assumed the
heaven and the earth to be divided by an impassable
chasm. "It is the spirit", He said, "that giveth life,
the flesh profiteth nothing: the sayings which I have
spoken unto you are spirit and are life". "But", he
added, "there are of you,"—you, my disciples,—
"some who believe not";—some, that is, who have no
sense of the invisible; men to whom loaves of bread
are much but Divine sayings are nothing, because
spirit is nothing, and life apart from its concrete
manifestations is nothing. The sayings which He
had been speaking to them could not but be unsub-
stantial indeed in eyes to which flesh was the standard
of substance: their true substance was the substance
of spirit, which is the proper realm of life, and therefore they too were lifegiving to eyes whose sight was
the sight of faith.

Here we have the teaching of the Speaker of the
lifegiving sayings Himself. Immediately afterwards
we have the testimony of those disciples in whom
distrust of the unseen had failed at least to obtain
the mastery. When many of the disciples departed
and went back, and walked no more with Jesus, He
said to the Twelve, "Have ye also a will to go your
way?" St Peter answered, "Lord, unto whom shall
we depart? sayings hast thou of eternal life: and we
have believed and come to know that thou art the
Holy One of God." If we are careful not to read
into this bold and yet restricted profession the mature

beliefs of a later time, we may learn much from it
concerning the nature of the life which was found in
the Lord. Discipleship could no longer be thought
of as a terminable interruption to ordinary employ-
ments: for weal or woe, it had become the primary
occupation. And further the present discipleship
admitted of no other to succeed it. Some at least of
the Twelve had in a manner 'departed' from John
the Baptist when they came to Christ: but no fresh
departure of the same kind was possible. The Baptist
himself had sanctioned that first departure, for he had
recognised that the new voice was the voice of the
Bridegroom, the voice of life and joy, the voice of
One who came not with a single rounded and com-
pleted office or message external to Himself, but
who must needs go on increasing. Even such a Lord
the Twelve had already found their Lord to be, in
spite of the stumbling-blocks which beset their feet
as they strove to walk with Him.

The adherence of the Twelve rested on surer
foundations than the recollection of having been fed
in the wilderness, or of the miraculous manner of the
feeding, though these had been helpful signs and
lessons. The reason why they could not depart from
the Lord was because He had spoken to them and
His voice had entered into them. His sayings had
been outpourings of a life which had wakened to
response the slumbering life within themselves. And
the life which they had thus felt kindling them they

had felt also to have the quality of eternity : whether
their own hold on it were fitful and fleeting or steady
and sure, it issued forth itself from a source too deep
for earthly ebb and flow, even from Him in whom all
is eternal. And so through this experience, hard to
translate but impossible to reason away, they had
passed beyond the sense of a benefit, beyond gratitude to a benefactor, into a faith, at once a vision
and an allegiance, which had already begun to unfold
itself into a growing knowledge. Already through
their Lord they had begun to know God more truly,
and simultaneously to know their Lord Himself in
relation to God as well as to themselves, to know
Him as the Holy One of God, God's chosen representative, the personal medium of a life which not
only was mighty and inspiring but purified while it
inspired, and tended ever upward and Godward in
its direction. Departure from a Lord known by such
tokens to possess such attributes, however His words
and deeds might perplex them, and however imperfectly they could formulate their own apprehensions
of His person, would, they well knew, be implicitly
nothing less than departure from God.

This submissive sense of personal life proceeding
from the Teacher and Lord, and especially as imparted through His sayings, is indeed in great measure
by no means peculiar. Similar outgoings of life and
receptions of life accompany the ordinary human
discipleships of all ages, for in this as in other

respects the discipleship to Christ is the ratification
and completion of all discipleships. Nay this is the
most precious element of discipleship, filial or other;
itself, when wisely ordered, an almost indispensable
condition of harmony of inward growth. Beside the
kindling of spirit at spirit, all efforts after independent self-stimulation and self-culture are weak, and
all instruments of stimulation and culture continued
and applied by others weaker still: and though the
kindling power is great even when exerted by equals,
it is greatest and least liable to misuse when it is in
some shape authoritative, arising out of a manifest
ascendancy at once functional and personal, to which
thought and feeling do grateful homage for the free
activities which they learn to put forth in yielding
to its sway.

Thus the possession and utterance of sayings of
eternal life is in its measure common to all great
spiritual teachers of things Divine. The distinctive
perception of the Twelve concerning their Teacher
and Lord consisted in this, that their personal experience of Him as the Lord of their own hearts and
minds was joined to a recognition of purposes, offices,
and powers in Him which ranged immeasurably beyond benefits conferred on themselves, and gave the
impression of being coextensive with the Providence
of God. The inward sense of life imparting life was
necessary probably to the very existence of this recognition, certainly to its vividness and operative

8—2

force. Yet by itself it could not reach to discerning
the uniqueness of the Life-giver: it was through the
concurring glimpses of His loftiness and His universality that He could be named, in such wise as He
then was named, the Holy One of God.

The unclean spirits had instantly called Him by
the same name, for they too perceived that He was
come from God to put in force the holiness of God,
and this it was that roused their terror at His presence. The disciples learned its truth only by
degrees; but they found in it the sufficient reason
why they should cleave to His presence when others
were departing, and when the impulse to depart was
felt within themselves too. They could not think of
the eternal life which they felt within themselves as
separable from Him who had awakened it, or His
uplifting power over themselves from His kingly
representation of the Holy and Living God.

The departure which had been spoken of at that
close of one time of probation was a departure of the
disciples from the Lord. The perplexity which found
vent in St Thomas's question on the evening of the
Last Supper arose out of the impending departure
of the Lord from the disciples. In the interval the
sayings of eternal life had taken fuller possession,
though not yet able to banish doubt and misgiving.
Among them were the words with which He had
guided Martha to better thoughts than those with

which she had met Him on the way to the grave of
Lazarus, saying to her " I am the Resurrection and
the Life ". On the one side were the jealous individual attachment which claimed the Lord only for
herself and her brother, and the confidence in His
power to prevail with God which assumed that His
advocacy would be set in motion in like manner by
individual friendship rather than by all-embracing
allegiance to the Father's will : on the other was the
languid expectation, accepted passively from the prevailing creed, that in some distant time her brother
should rise again, and the inability to be satisfied
with a promise too widely detached from the sorrow-
ful present to affect deeply the sense of death within.
Both sets of feelings were purified and enlarged together. The personal attachment was expanded into
a faith which could recognise the individual heart's
Lord as the universal Lord : the torpid expectation
was quickened into a living hope by becoming rooted
in a personal faith. The truth of resurrection could be
learned only through the truth of life, and the truth of
life could be learned only in the Living One in whom
life in all its modes is summed up from the beginning.
He was the Resurrection because He was the Life.
Faith in Him was for men itself the primary resurrection, and in the light of that faith alone could the
hope of every other resurrection be true and sure.

Thus when our Lord said to the disciples in the
upper room " I am the Life ", the designation ex-

pressed not only the fundamental truth towards which
many thoughts of theirs had under His guidance
long been tending, but had itself been uttered in
their hearing no long time before, and that in a
combination which gave it a peculiar force now that
the threatenings of hostile Jews, joined with His own
earlier predictions of His fate at the hands of men
and His present language about departure, were to
their eyes casting over Him a shadow too like the
shadow of death. As He spoke not now of death
but of a journey, so neither did He speak now of
resurrection : nothing was allowed to disguise the
continuity and the true issue of the journey, coming
to the Father ; or to impair by secondary applications
the simple breadth of the teaching which by means
of this crisis the chosen apostles were appointed to
receive. Yet though at such a season the word " I
am the Life " involved even a greater paradox than
its predecessors, it was also better fitted to instil
strength into the sinking hearts of disciples by the
bare force of its contrast with anticipated death, and
still more by its association with the answer given to
Martha, and with the signs following after by which
authority over the realm of death had been victori-
ously maintained.

The announcement came however as the last of
three : we have to read it neither as a repetition of
what had been spoken to Martha nor yet absolutely
but as the third step in the self-revelation of our

Lord to St Thomas in response to his anxious questioning. The disciple had no need to enquire by what way the Lord was going, or by what way He might be followed hereafter, if only his discipleship had already led him to a true knowledge of his Lord, and especially prepared him to see his Lord as the one universal Way for all the goings of man.

Yet even this recognition would be found insufficient when brought face to face with a maturer and more reflective experience. The goings of men, the movements of events within and around men, are after all in one sense derivative, not primary. They are conditioned by the permanent constitution and relations of men without and within, and after a certain stage of growth men's goings need for their regulation a knowledge of these relations and [this] constitution. A way presupposes a truth, and knowledge of truth sooner or later becomes indispensable for walking in a right way. Hence Christ's claim to be called the Way required for its substantiation an equal claim to be called the Truth. Discipleship to Him had throughout its course involved perpetual manifestation of truth and perpetual education of the power of apprehending truth, and that in close relation to Himself. And so on the one hand its office in the future would vitally depend on perpetual apprehension of truth, and on the other Christ the Word of God, by virtue of his primary relation to all created things, would be found to be the Truth of truth, and

knowledge of Him to be the keystone of all knowledge.

But again these two responses to the perplexed
disciple by no means fill up the sum of need of which
experience makes him conscious. Man and the
universe surrounding man can by no means be re-
solved completely into a succession of acts and events
and a constitutive order of permanent forms. The one
most mysterious but most mighty factor of created
things remains, the link between the two worlds of
movement and of order, even that which generalising
rudely from a single conspicuous manifestation we
call life, and for which philosophy has found no
better name. It reaches in unbroken range from the
obscurest marshallings of the inner substance of
seemingly lifeless things up to the loftiest exaltations
of the human spirit. This life as it is in man, partly
shared with the lower animals, partly unique, not
only is the necessary latent base of human action and
knowledge, but by their side and in their midst has
its own proper manifestations in what is called in the
widest sense emotion. Life is more than emotion,
but the special expression of life is emotion.

Here then was a world within man, his very
innermost world, which had to learn its own proper
form of discipleship. If right ways are hard to find,
if the truth of things is hard to be known, yet harder
is it to attain to an order in the obscure chaos of
feeling, to bring it into harmonious cooperation with

the other human energies, nay to keep it from de-
ranging or subverting their work. And yet its presence has no mere natural necessity, to be accepted
but not to be cherished. If it touched the lowest in
man, it was also itself his highest, and a bond between
his highest and his lowest. The agencies that had
tended and were still tending to estrange the Eleven
from Christ were not merely rival ways in which they
were tempted to walk, or rival teachings which they
were tempted to accept as presentations of truth.
More than all these were rival distractions of their
life through the witcheries of life's power, or even the
claims of its seeming authority; distractions belonging partly to the natural life of impulse found in all
the higher orders of living creatures, partly to the
life of human relationships, partly to the life belonging to the recognition of God. And as we have
already seen, what most enabled the Eleven to hold
steadfastly on in spite of these distractions was the
timid yet clear response of the life within them to the
commanding Life in their midst. Into this region
their questioning minds must now be conducted that
the final decision might be securely made. The
choice of ways was arbitrary, the problem of truth
was insoluble, until council had been held in the
inner shrine of life.

The three steps in Christ's self-revelation to St
Thomas correspond therefore to the three great pro-
vinces of human energy generally, and likewise to

the three forms of discipleship which together consti-
tuted the personal education of the apostles during
the Lord's ministry; and in leading the apostles from
the way about which they were enquiring to the
knowledge of truth involved in any trustworthy acceptance of a way, and thence further down to the
testimony of life concerning life, He was conforming
to the order of universal fact exemplified in their
immature but unperverted natures. This ultimate
appeal however to the voice of life could be right,
nay strictly speaking could be possible, only in so
far as life was taught by the Truth, and exercised in
the Way. For it would be a fatal error to think of
the several characters which our Lord here attributes
to Himself, or the corresponding departments of
human nature either in the apostles or in any other
men, as separate and mutually exclusive. Distinguish the parts of human nature as we may, it
remains a living whole; and thus its indestructible
integrity is never inert in any action of any part,
while neglect or attempted suppression of it always
leads to perilous disaster. The higher the life in man
rises, the more need it has of knowledge to bestow
discrimination and proportion, and of ordered action
to bestow inward discipline and outward direction.

On the one hand life in its lower forms is the
common ground out of which action and knowledge
have sprung, and remains always their hidden condition. In its higher forms on the other hand life

outreaches action and knowledge. Yet all the pro-
perly human ascent and progress of life has been
dependent on progress in ways of action and in
knowledge ; and even the highest life, when it strives
to be independent of action and knowledge, loses all
claim to have a commanding voice for the will, and
tends downwards towards the helpless elements of
blind nature. The life in the disciples would be able
to recognise Christ as the very Life, because it was
the life of men whose reason demanded truth and
whose conscience demanded a supreme way. What
was deepest in them could close with what was
deepest in Him, because no conflict between different
parts of their true selves was involved, nay rather
they found a new harmony counteracting the solvent
distractions of trouble and sin.

Thus the unity of the Lord's three revealed characters in His own Person, was presented to the
disciples as the foundation for unity within themselves, while in each character He offered Himself as
the adequate satisfaction of the corresponding need.
If He were not the Life, it was little that He should
be the Way and the Truth. If it was only the outer
circles of human existence that found their true
purpose in His lordship and partook of His unity,
then the present had no order and the future no
promise. An independence of personality and affections and desires in each individual disciple, beneath
the common subjection to the one Way and the

one Truth, would have made discipleship at last a
mockery. He as the Life must rule their life at its
centre, if life and knowledge and action were to make
one harmonious whole. As their life was a life of
men, and was designed to enable them to do their
part among men, he must also be the life of mankind.
Once more, since the life of man is the summing up
of all lower lives, and implicitly includes them within
itself, He must be the Life of all creatures that live,
the First and the Last of all creation.

In the discourses of the last evening life is named
but once after the announcement of the Life to St
Thomas. Yet almost every sentence henceforth is a
teaching concerning life as it is at its highest. The
word which immediately gathers up the three announcements, "No man cometh unto the Father save
through me", though moulded by the initial conception of the Way, in its inner sense interprets the Way
by the Life. Translated into any language but that
of the aspiring life of love, 'coming to the Father' is
a hollow and dangerous phrase: as pronounced by
the Son, it proclaims the ultimate source of life in
the Father's eternal Fatherhood.

St Philip's appeal, " Lord, shew us the Father and
it sufficeth us ", was a response of reawakened though
still ill-instructed life; and our Lord's answer to it
aims at drawing forth into clearness this its latent
ground. He explains the assurance, " He that hath

seen me hath seen the Father", by suggesting what
manner of vision it is that must fill the eye of a
disciple's heart. "Believest thou not that I am in
the Father and the Father is in me?" Here is life
in its first and eternal movement, the union and
communion of the Father and the Son. Hence flows
in created things all their life, always resting on union
and communion, always tending upwards towards
the perfect spiritual union and communion within the
Godhead. In proportion as created things become
able to know their life, and to know it in its divine
fountain, they learn to recognise the manifestations
of the Father's mind in the Son's words and works,
and in that light to recognise them in all things.
"The sayings which I speak to you I speak not of
mine own self, but the Father abiding in me doeth
His works". Those very sayings which carried
eternal life to the disciples' hearts were works of the
Father abiding and working in the Son. Their experience of that life was untrue to itself if it failed to
inspire faith, a faith not to be quenched by aught
that might befall the outward form and voice through
which they had known their Lord, but going forward
to rest through Him on the living God.

The next portion of the discourse has for its chief
subject love, that is, that joyful sense of recognised
union and communion which is the culmination of
life. The disciples' genuine love to the Lord was in
danger of becoming the excuse for blank dismay at

His departure: it was in danger also of resting within itself instead of spending itself upon fit result. Therefore the homely warning came, "If ye love me, ye will keep my commandments". Here was the principle: love to be worthy the name must be love at work, love governed by duty. But the original perplexity at once presented itself afresh in a new shape: how was the principle to be put in force without higher guidance? "I will ask the' Father, and He will give you another Advocate that He may be with you for ever, even the Spirit of the Truth". For the moment it sufficed to announce this new and inward Advocate, Who was henceforth to teach the love of the present Advocate how to go forth into action as the keeping of His commandments through increasing knowledge of His Truth. Christ then returned to the wound which He seemed to be inflicting on the love to Himself. "I will not leave you bereaved, I come unto you. Yet a little while and the world beholdeth me no more: but ye behold me, because I live, and ye shall live. In that day ye yourselves shall come to know that I am in my Father, and ye in Me, and I in you". The departure was to be real, but it was not to be the whole reality. In the midst of their desolation they should behold Him coming to them, and that first new coming out of the darkness of death should be the pledge and type of comings which should meet their longing eyes in many a future desolation. These comings should indeed be invisible to the outward sense, to the powers of sight that they possessed in common with 'the world', and that were compatible with that death of the higher nature which was characteristic of 'the world'. The eyes which should recognise His coming would be organs generated by the growth of life: Him the Living One the disciples should see, because they too should be quickened with His own eternal and yet risen life. In that day of revelation, no longer by the hearing of the ear but by the light of a sympathetic experience of their own, they should learn the hidden origin and course of life and of love, even the primary union and communion of the Son with the Father, and the derivative union and communion of disciples with the Son.

The second great division of these discourses begins with a longer and less interrupted withdrawal from the region of present perplexities into the invisible and fixed personal relationship of which the whole present trouble was an incident. Christ declared Himself now to be the true vine of which His Father was the husbandman and His disciples the branches. He imaged Himself as Israel's own sacred tree of life, alike by its glorious growths and by the gladdening energy of its produce a true and hallowed type of abounding life. He turned the disciples away from that visible and obvious relation to each other and to Him which consisted in distinctness and detachment; teaching them to recognise that in the

inner region of life all several centres and person-
alities find their base and their complement in an
underlying unity; teaching them also in the same
breath that He was not a partaker of the unity but
its source and its pervading embodiment. He the
Life was not one among many branches but the tree
of which all the branches were subordinate out-
growths. While they were in the vine their life
subsisted: if they suffered themselves to be detached
from the vine, their life must perish. To 'abide'
therefore in the vine was their first necessity and
duty; and the counterpart of it was the fulfilment of
the function of a vine-branch, the bearing of fruit.
A life which bore no good fruit was a perverted life,
and barren branches would in the Husbandman's eye
be excrescences which He must needs take away.
Nay each branch itself needed the cleansing away of
its own excrescences that it might bear more fruit.
But beside this outer cleansing by trouble, such as it
was the Father's purpose that the disciples should
now undergo, there was a more effectual cleansing by
the power of a divine life within. Already that power
had wrought in them to good effect: already the
eternal life residing in the Word which He had
spoken to them had cast off many a barren excres-
cence which had seemed part of themselves. What
remained was to suffer no detachment from the
central Life, and to treasure in the chambers of
living hearts the sayings of life which had entered

into them, the many partial utterances of the one
word or revelation of life, that they might be always
means of fresh renewal and consummation to the
lifelong discipleship. Yet it was no ecstasy of
dreaming recluses that was enjoined or promised,
but love and obedience, the simplest ruling elements
of a true and pure human life, consecrated by the
revelation of their patterns in the heavens. "As the
Father loved me, I also loved you: abide ye in my
love. If ye keep my commandments, ye shall abide
in my love, as I have kept my Father's commandments, and abide in His love."

This is the theme which under various applications,
speaking much to the present and yet more to the
future, is pursued through many verses. With love,
the highest manifestation of life, Christ now associates
joy, its never-failing accompaniment, not as a thing
given by His power but as flowing from His person,
that it may meet and complete and substantiate the
incoherent and precarious joy which they had known
already. "These things have I spoken to you that
my joy may be in you, and your joy may be fulfilled."
Then He passes on at once to the issue and trial of
love, which was also a lesson in the character and
method of His own joy. To abide in His love involved the loving of one another. As at the beginning
of the conversation, He treats this mutual love as no
ready product of spontaneous impulse, but as the
fulfilment of a searching precept which needed to be

spoken with emphatic authority: "this is my commandment that ye love one another as I loved you."
The test of a love having this origin was self-sacrifice.
In all its grades it could be tried by reference to that
perfect fruit of it which He was shewing forth in
laying down His soul for their sake.

The love then from which the promised joy was
inseparable might lead of necessity to the uttermost
suffering. Hatred on the part of the world without,
which had broken forth against Him and His Father,
would not fail to pursue the brotherhood of His
disciples. They must not suffer themselves to stumble
at these consequences of following Him in His love.
The already promised Advocate, whose name is the
Spirit of the Truth, should by His coming renew the
presence of the vanished Advocate and Lord in deeper
and ampler power. The witness which He should
bear to their hearts concerning Christ should enable
them to bear their own appointed witness of word and
act in the face of persecution. Though they were as
yet unable to carry the weight of the many things
which He had still to say to them, what they had
already seen and heard in the days during which
they had been with Him would fully suffice, when
wrought out for them by the Spirit of the Truth in
adaptation to each several need. Though it is of
truth and the knowledge of truth that our Lord
speaks directly here, the context shews that He had
in view an office of the Spirit in regard to the Life

analogous to His interpretative office in regard of the
Truth, and indeed closely accompanying it. It was
only through the successive breathings of the Life-
giving Spirit of the Truth throughout the ages that
the Life-giving Lord should yield for human use the
virtue of His one and abiding life. Neither could
that life of His be ever without His truth, nor His
truth without His life. He expands His first words
about guidance into the Truth, and about the Spirit
as speaking' only what He hears, into a promise
inclusive of every thing Divine that is communicable
to man. "He", the Spirit of the Truth, "shall
glorify me, for He shall take of what is mine and
declare it to you: all things whatsoever the Father
hath are mine; therefore said I that He taketh of
what is mine and shall declare it to you."

In expounding the mysterious trouble of the
present, the Lord had of necessity lifted forward the
discourse into the high responsibilities of days to
come. So alone could He bring a solace which
should be also a strengthening, effectual at last, if
not at once, because dealing with that life which is
also light. But He would not leave it possible for
the disciples to misinterpret this deliberate method
of His consolation as a forgetfulness of their distress.
He returned therefore to the burden of His first
announcements, "a little while and ye behold me no
more, and again a little while and ye shall see me";
and when the words were found still hard to interpret,

He instructed the disciples to look on their impending sorrows as the travail-pangs of a mighty birth into the world, and therefore the necessary prelude of a joy to themselves of which no power external to themselves could rob them. He promised as the characteristic of that new day an open and trustful communion with the Father through Himself, a sharing, that is, in His own inmost filial life, in which the offering of prayer in His name and the granting of prayer in His name should be the fulfilment of joy. For a moment He chastened the too confidently professed faith in the completeness of His knowledge and the Divine origin of His mission, in spite of which the disciples would shortly suffer their present communion with Him and with each other to be for the while dissolved, and would leave Him, as far as act of theirs could reach, alone; as nearly alone as was possible to One whose communion with the Father was unbroken. But the rebuke of premature confidence that trusted in itself enforced yet more strongly the need and the power of the sustaining life to be drawn from communion with His life. With a promise of peace in Him amid conflict, of victory in Him amid defeat, as the ordained result of receiving these His sayings, the discourse ends.

Within the first petition of the prayer which our Lord sent forth with uplifted eyes into the heaven eternal life is once more named : " Father, the hour is come : glorify Thy Son, that the Son may glorify

Thee, as Thou gavest Him right over all flesh, that, every thing which Thou hast given Him, He should give to them eternal life." In perfecting the work which the Father had given Him to do, the Son already glorified the Father on the earth. But a consummation of received and reflected glory in death and resurrection was still to come ; and it was measured by the breadth of the heritage bestowed on the Son as the Son of Man. Not disciples only but all flesh, every thing which the Father had given as part of the heritage, was destined to share the Son's eternal life, as it already shared a lower life in Him ; and that gift of eternal life was to grow out of His own glorious perfecting. "And this", He said, "is the eternal life, that they know Thee, the only true God, and Him whom Thou didst send, Jesus Christ." The words have already been cited as implying certain characteristics of the Truth : their direct purport concerns us even more now by what it declares on the other hand respecting that higher or spiritual life which decays not like the life of the grass, but has a share in eternity. It is no blind clinging to an unknown power in the upper abysses, but itself conditioned by knowledge and the abiding pursuit of knowledge. This vital knowledge stops not short of the Highest : its supreme object is God ; God ascertained by the light of truth as against all figments of the heart or mind which usurp His awful Name. And the word "Thee" determines this true

God : the true God is He whom Jesus called " Father",
He therefore whom Jesus was revealing by perfect
sonship upon earth. Thus the knowledge of God is
involved in the knowledge of Jesus recognised as His
Christ ; and the eternal life is lived when every power
takes hold of the manifested Life who is also the
manifested Light.

In the prayer, as in the discourse which it crowned,
the naming of life is succeeded by various sayings
bearing on relations to the Lord which can be
understood only as relations of life. The most
characteristic sentences are the petitions, first for the
disciples, and then for those who believe through the
disciples' word, that they may be all one ; " one", He
prays, " as thou, Father, in me and I in thee, that
they themselves also may be in us"; and again, " I
in them and thou in me, that they all may be perfected into one, that the world may know that thou
didst send me, and didst love them as thou didst love
me". By the concluding words, as by the words of
like import in the similitude of the Vine and the
branches, the life to which this unity and this communion belong is made known through the human
experience of love : and the same strain is repeated
in the last words of the prayer, uttered just before
the Lord went out with the disciples towards the
garden : " I made known to them thy Name and will
make it known that the love wherewith thou lovedst
me may be in them and I in them." Through the

mystery of love Christ's disciples were given an
entrance into the mystery of life; and it was by the
present and future knowledge of Christ's love, not
originating in Himself but carrying on the Father's
love to Him, that Christ's disciples were more and
more to know the Life, to be filled with it, and to
manifest it themselves for the salvation of the world.

The discourse and the prayer were the last prelude
to that signal revelation of the life of God bestowed
on man which is the cardinal event in the history of
mankind as it was in that of the disciples. Perfect
love, the surest characteristic of perfect life, was
wrought and shewn in the sacrifice of the Cross.
Nothing less than that consummation at once of love
and of obedience could heal the inveterate breach
which sin had made in the life of man; and moreover
the Life itself could not be victorious for man till it
had gone down into death and come forth again as
the Resurrection. When the Death in which the
Sacrifice culminated was found to issue not in the
extinction of life but in its transference to an invisible
sphere of existence, revealed to disciples at chosen
seasons of visibility, it was no longer guessed but
known that life in man could outlive the terrestrial
frame which had been from birth at once its product
and its mother. And since He whom God had thus
raised out of the dead was that very chosen Holy
One of His whose words and deeds had seemed
pregnant with fulfilment of all God's promises to His

people, and whose grave had thus seemed to be the grave of all hopes, every promise became sealed anew from above, and every hope rose up into an undying life in indissoluble union with the risen Lord. The things of old time had passed away: behold they were become new.

When on the Day of Pentecost the external signs of the Holy Spirit's presence were followed by other signs consisting of praises uttered in strange speech among the disciples, the bystanders exclaimed, "They are filled with new wine". The mocking comment was true. In the early days of the Church at Jerusalem the new wine of life overflows the doings of the disciples and the words of their spokesmen.

> "I foresaw the Lord in my presence alway,
> How that He is on my right hand that I may not be shaken:
> Therefore did my heart rejoice and my tongue exult;
> Yea and my flesh also shall rest in hope;
> For thou wilt not forsake my soul unto Hades,
> Neither wilt thou give Thy Holy One to see corruption;
> Thou madest known to me ways of life,
> Thou shalt fill me with gladness before Thy face."

In these measured strains of the ancient hymn the foremost of the apostles declares to the men of Israel at their Pentecostal feast the new mind which was entering into the disciples of Jesus now that God had loosed the travail-pangs of death. Every note is a note of exulting life, and this life as of old,—rather, far more than of old,—lives only by its hold upon the mighty and living God. What had been hoped was

now known. God had first revealed His Holy One,
and then out of the lowest depths had exalted Him
by His own right hand; and the promise fulfilled to
Him was pronounced anew in Him to His brethren,
the partakers of His holiness.

The circumstances under which the disciples received the ancient life thus renewed and enlarged
marked it out as a distinctive possession of their own.
As they spoke of "this Way", so also they spoke of
"this Life". So only can we rightly understand the
angel's words, "Go and stand and speak in the temple
to the people all the sayings of this life." His words
imply no less that it was the glory of the chosen few
to proclaim this life of theirs as held by no private
ownership. Such indeed was the tenour of St Peter's
language from the first: "to you is the promise, and
to your children, and to all that are afar off, even as
many as the Lord our God shall call to Him." On the
other hand the fruits of life were shown in the young
society of the Christian brotherhood. Communion
as a principle of life was embodied in the voluntary
community of goods, a visible sign of the leaven with
which it was to be the office of the Church to leaven
all social relations. The temple and the household
were alike sacred places where life was daily renewed
for daily thoughts and words and deeds. Life in its
lower forms was gratefully honoured as the sign and
foundation of life in its higher forms: "they that
believed partook of food in exultation and simplicity

of heart, praising God and having grace toward all
the people." The first external act of which we hear
is a continuation of Christ's own ministration of
bodily life : the Christian gift of vital power was
displayed in contrast to the earthly gift of dead
possessions when Peter said to the lame beggar at
the temple gate " Silver and gold have I none, but
what I have, this give I thee ", and immediately he
entered with the apostles" into the temple walking
and leaping and praising God. And here and always
the ascended Lord was believed on as in the midst,
giving forth out of Himself every distributed portion
of life : whatsoever was done was done in the name
of Jesus Christ.

This was the bright beginning. But the life of
disciples of Jesus could not reach its own perfection
or fulfil its due tasks without the stress of suffering.
Persecutions quickly came, imprisonments and scourg-
ing, with threats of death ; and thus arose a clear
perception that for the servants, as for the Master,
human enmity and resistance would be God's instruments in accomplishing His counsel, a simple prayer
to speak God's word with all boldness, and a joy
that they, witnesses of the Name, were counted
worthy to suffer dishonour for the Name. At length
the testimony had to be perfected in blood, as the
consistent result of owning Jesus the Crucified as
Lord ; and, following Him by the same way, Stephen
died with words of faith and forgiveness on his lips

which disclose the calm and sane energy of his heart.

Fierce persecution and dispersion ensued ; and from that time forward, admitted to fellowship with the sufferings of God's Christ, the disciples were enabled to learn what they had but imperfectly known on that last evening. They learned to give their life freely away, because this was the ever present condition under which they could fulfil His work, and because the ultimate future of their life depended not on any power inherent in itself, but on Him who died and rose again. Respites of comparative peace were accorded them from time to time : but the intervals were few when danger, suffering, and death were not at work to strengthen and purify the apostolic life which was to be the human attestation of the Gospel.

Throughout the teaching of the apostles, as preserved in their epistles, life, named or unnamed, is found the chief moving power and the chief good that is desired. Its fervour and its peace make up the common element which holds together the varied instructions and exhortations elicited by the various needs of the Churches, and unites them all to the personal experience of the apostles themselves. It sustains alike the doctrine and the ethics which were the necessary subjects of teaching : and in its heights the doctrine and the ethics are merged at last. It appears under three principal forms, as faith, as hope, and as love ;—faith in the unseen God, creating a

Divine righteousness in the midst of accusing memories of broken laws; hope in the counsel of God, looking forward through present distresses and perplexities to the accomplishment of His glorious purpose; and love answering the love of God, outglowing and dissolving the prides and hatreds and meaner desires which gender desolation and death without and within, and finding the guiding principle of action between man and man in stewardship of the manifold grace of God for the manifold service of the Kingdom of God.

That the teaching of the apostles should be chiefly concerned with life at its highest, the eternal life, the life indeed, was a necessary result of their special work. But both the substance and the form of their moral exhortations exclude its detachment from the lower stages of life by which ordinary human society is animated. They take their stand on the primary relations of mankind, and the emotions which accompany their right fulfilment. They slight no part of the composite nature of man, but claim the whole for Divine use and Divine glory. If their teaching is unique in its elevation, it is equally unique in the compass of its unity.

The aspects of life under the pressure of death became better known to the apostles when the trials and sufferings of the Church and its leaders were gathering into one great crisis. At an earlier time St Paul had already poured forth his own recent

acquaintance with that twofold lore in his second
epistle to the Corinthians, the most expressive record
of a profoundly Christian soul for whom the middle
world of ordinary thoughts and doings became for
the while well-nigh invisible by the upsurging of the
deeps of the spirit through a tempest of affliction.
When persecution increased, other apostolic writers
had each his own word of life through death to speak.
But when at last the Day of the Lord came in its
extremest terrors, a yet clearer message was delivered by the beloved disciple in the " Revelation of
Jesus Christ" with which he taught and comforted
the seven churches of Asia in the strength of the
passionate life of martyrdom. The voice of the
Martyr Faithful and True, the Slain Lamb, who is
also the First and the Last and the Living One, goes
sounding through the book. To him who conquers,
faithful in his doings as well as his sufferings, is a
promise given that he shall eat of the tree of life,
that tree whose leaves are for the healing of the
nations, and shall wear the victor's festive crown of
life. He whose blood had been the ransom to loose
His servants from their sins was both their power and
their pattern as they entered into the depths of His
faithful witnessing: "they themselves conquered "
the Accuser "because of the blood of the Lamb and
because of the word of their witnessing, and they
loved not their soul unto death". Yet He who was
thus to His suffering witnesses the pledge and source

of life, to His enemies the stern warrior Judge, to all
the King of kings and Lord of lords, was called the
Word of God. In all things He was the Speech of
God to men ; no mere Giver or mere Gift, but the
supreme Revealer, the Way and the Truth, in short,
as well as the Life.

That Day of the Lord passed away; and the
apostle and prophet who had been its interpreter
lived on into the next generation. No search is
needed to learn from the epistle which he wrote to
his 'children' towards the end of his days whether
he had found it true that Jesus Christ was the Life.
He begins by assuming that all his own converse
with his Lord in the flesh by hearing and sight and
touch was concerning the Word or revelation of the
Life. "And the Life", he proceeds, "was manifested,
and we have seen, and we bear witness and announce
to you the Life, the eternal Life, even that Life
which was with the Father and was manifested to
us." He declares the purpose of the announcement
to be communion, communion with the Father and
the Son through the apostolic witnesses ; and the
purpose of his present writing he declares to be the
fulfilment of joy. The Son of God, come in the flesh,
holds a similar place in St John's exposition of love,
the chief ethical theme of his epistle. He sets aside
all human pretensions which dispense with love; not
a nominal love of God which bears no such fruit as
that by which God's own love is known to us, but a

love which goes forth upon men as God's love went forth in the life and death of His Son: and at the same time he represents this genuine love toward God and men as having no separate existence, but as being simply the love of the Father and the Son entering into man and abiding and working in him. Before the epistle closes, the substance of the opening words is repeated with graver emphasis. "And this is the witness, that God gave us eternal life, and this life is in His Son. · He that hath the Son hath the Life, he that hath not the Son of God hath not the Life. These things I write to you that ye may know that ye have eternal life, even to you that believe on the name of the Son of God." The surpassing preciousness of life, the fundamental unity of life, and the identity of the incarnate Son of God with the Life as One, these are the crowning convictions which rose up for the aged apostle above all the other teaching of long and troubled years, and with which he strove to arm his 'children' against the keenly presaged dangers of the coming age in which the last apostolic voice should be still.

Yet more explicit evidence comes to us from the book which was to be the vehicle of his witness concerning what he had seen and heard to every generation which should be willing to enter through his witness into his communion with the Father and the Son. We have already seen how emphatically he there pronounces life to be the appointed fruit of faith, and

faith to be the appointed fruit of the Incarnation;
and declares at the close that with a view to this
twofold end he had written his narrative of the
Incarnation. His Prologue enables us to see his
conception of life and of the Life in its full breadth.
Of the Word, who was in the beginning with GOD,
and was God, he says, with reference to the initial
and perpetual coming of all things into being through
Him, that in Him was life, and the Life was the
Light of men. What He specially was as the Light
to men, as beings endowed with the power of knowing
truth, had its source, so to speak, in what He was as
the Life not of them only but of all finite things.
That which gave to all things whatsoever they had of
form and order and unity and motion and function
was their life, and that life was but the multitudinous
efflux of Him the Life. This designation best expressed the most comprehensive relation in which He
stood to the universe who is the Word of GOD, the
eternal fundamental utterance of HIM whose diffracted
and remoter utterance is the universe. In the same
breath with these announcements of primary mysteries
St John goes on to language which shews how far he
had been from forgetting human blindness and sin
and their Divine remedies. His recital of the progress of the Word through history is interwoven with
tragic intimations how the darkness apprehended not
the Light shining in it, how the world knew not the
Word through whom it came into being, how, when

He came into His own, they who were His own
received Him not. The seemingly remote fields of
view are brought together when he comes to speak
of the results of the Incarnation. The Apostles had
beheld His glory, a glory as of an only-begotten from
a father, the manifestation doubtless of those attributes which the opening verses had recounted. As a
dweller among men He had been recognised as full
of grace and truth, in such wise that they who knew
Him could not doubt that His was the fulness out of
which we all had received whatever portion of grace
and truth we possessed. Nay, as the Law was given
through Moses, so the Grace and the Truth, the
human derivations from the Life above and the Light
above, came into being through Jesus Christ. Thus
the power of life and the power of truth which had
made themselves felt throughout His earthly course,
the characteristics which stamped Him as the Saviour
and the Revealer, were antecedent to human sin and
error; they were involved in the original relations of
the Word of God to the universe of God. And so
the eternal life which St John held forth as generated
by faith in the Incarnate Son was linked in his
teaching to the whole scale of life in man and in the
creatures less living than man, because he knew that
all life is one in Him whose word spoken originally
to Thomas he had now an enlarged capacity to
receive. The life-giving Spirit had illumined for him
that once dark word, till it had become the last

message out of the fulness of the apostolic experience, the eagerly commended pledge that the communion vouchsafed to apostles was open through them to their disciples to the end of time.

The call to the disciples to receive Christ unreservedly as the Life is a call which surely the Church of later days may well accept as addressed to itself.

Not without anxious effort can we learn that by God's decree the first stage of discipleship is over. Christ Himself before long will assuredly cease to be in any sense our life, if we look for His life only in the form of a private affection or in isolation from the lower life which we share with all living things and the varied relationships by which we are united to our fellow-men. It is the glory of His life to include every life. We do not purify it but impoverish it by detracting from its fulness. It may be that all lower forms of life are rising and will rise yet more in rebellion against the life of Christ as though it were only a cunningly disguised death. Yet the Church will be false to herself and to the universality of the task committed to her if she seeks to protect the life of Christ by striving to fence it round into a little province of peculiar emotion. There is indeed that in it which is known only to those who have most communed with the living Lord Himself, and been baptized by Him with a holy spirit and with fire. Yet it ceases to be His life when it ceases to go forth and save. It was ordained to purify and control every lower life; and therefore it must enter freely into them all. If we fear that it may lose itself in the vast and often lawless universe of life beneath, the danger is to be averted not by wilfully contracting it within a narrower field, but by seeking greater intensity of life in deeper and more submissive communion with the Head Himself in the heavens.

Again, there is a season in the lifetime of each of us when all that the word 'life' expresses has a greater charm for us than any other good thing, though it is then that all good things are poured out before us in the richest abundance. Life seems to flow bounteously within us and around us, and we are slow to tolerate any restraints upon its exuberance. Many things which are then good in our eyes are permitted to draw us away from Him whom the Gospel calls our Life; and at best we find the stream of our inner self divided into many a mazy current. Yet if this inward distraction continues, the life which we prize is condemned to be fleeting in duration and fruitless in result. Now more than ever have we need of the one master Life to take possession of us and of all His gifts to us. Now more than ever must we hold fast the faith, which experience will ratify in due time that our own desires are less the ministers than the destroyers of life until they are subdued into glad obedience to His holy and hallowing Will, the Will of the Life that was crucified and rose again from the dead.

If it is becoming harder than it once was to accept His life as one life among many, the change to a clearer issue is one that all who believe in Him may welcome. It cannot be truly known as life at all till it is known as the Supreme Life. If other lives will not be ruled by His life, they must presently seek to cast it out as an evil thing. Wherever they for the time prevail, they work perdition and destruction for a little hour, and then they perish while yet proving that life cannot be slighted or repudiated with impunity. Wherever He prevails, He conquers that He may save. Could His life be banished from the life of men, the bright heathen life that once lived in ages long preceding His coming could live no more as it lived then. The ancient gods, the gods of the earth, were not slain by the Nazarene. They were dead and mouldering long before the Eternal Son came down from heaven and was born of the Blessed Virgin's womb. He destroyed nothing that had life: He lives that all which once lived may live again in Him. No ancient form of life can perish for ever, though it be long before mankind are fitted to receive it back at Christ's hands, renewed and transfigured by His resurrection.

As it is with the youth of mankind, so it is with

the youth of each and all. If the season is past when
nature ministers life abundantly, yet He who died to
nature that He might live to God has a saving power
in store for every season. If He is sought, not as a
residuary solace because life has failed, or only as
holding the keys of a dim and distant future, but as
Himself the Life and eternal life, He will open hidden
springs of life in the desert within and the deserts
around, that what remains of the threescore years
and ten may be moulded into a living form, fair in
His eyes and fit for His service. Old works of death
and darkness have to be cast off; the clogged channels
of life have to be sternly cleansed, the Baptist must
still prepare the way for the Saviour. But the
Saviour Himself stands always nigh to transform by
His presence the purifying water without into the
water of life, which is also the wine of gladness,
within. So He manifests His glory to His disciples.
So His disciples believe on Him, and live.

LECTURE IV.

No man cometh unto the Father but by Me.

THE earthly life and acts of the Lord, in Himself and in the Church of His disciples, are divided according to His own express teaching into two parts. Before the discourse of the Last Supper reaches its close, He opposes them to each other in sharp contrast. " I came out from the Father and am come into the world: again I leave the world and go unto the Father." When these two words of His are received in their distinctness and their mutual necessity, as setting forth at once historical fact and eternal truth, then the Gospel is embraced. To refuse both is to fall back into heathenism. To receive the first but let go the second, or to confuse the second with the first, is to retrace our steps and become once more believing Jews. To hold fast both together is to stand and move in the faith of Christ.

The first period is in its origin a coming forth, in its progress a descent. The Father or the Father's

presence is the beginning. The Son is sent forth
and Himself comes forth into the world which He
is to redeem. The weight of the world's sin and
misery lies on Him more and more. Each step in
His ministry brings Him into deadlier conflict with
the world; and as He goes steadily forward, the
conflict ends in His death. The Death belongs to
both periods. It is the lowest point of the descent,
the testimony sealed in blood, the obedience perfected
in sacrifice. But it is also the beginning of the ascent.
The Cross is already a lifting up out of the earth, a
prophecy of the lifting up into the heavens. God
accepts the sacrifice, raises His Son from the dead as
by a second birth, and exalts Him to sit at His own
right hand till He has put all His enemies under His
feet. By the descent is closed the long line of reve-
lations by which God came down and visited His
people Israel; by the ascent is announced and begun
the gathering of men upward to God, accomplished
once for all in the person of the Son of Man, and
wrought out through the ages in the power of that
first accomplishment.

In each of the two periods the presence of the
disciples is an essential part of the Gospel. Throughout the first period they are almost wholly receivers.
All elements of their discipleship are combined in
attachment to their Lord's person. They are being
prepared for a time when they will have to bear
witness of what they have seen and heard and known

of Him : and while this process is going on, He is acquiring a mastery over their whole nature, which is destined to disable them for a purely independent life hereafter.

After the Resurrection the passive discipleship continues in both respects under changed conditions. But the change is not fully manifest till the day of Pentecost, when they finally enter into that new stage of discipleship which is expounded throughout the discourse at the Last Supper on the eve of the Passion, discipleship being now fulfilled in apostleship. From that time forwards their work consists in the appropriation and distribution of His work. As the Father sent Him into the world, so He sent them into the world. Their destiny and their office are fashioned after His.

This double relation of the Lord's journey to the journey of the disciples shapes both parts of His answer to St Thomas. On the one hand it is for the sake of mankind that He takes His journey, and it is through men, learners from Him, that mankind are to be blessed by it. On the other hand it is on His own journey that both the possibility and the efficacy of the disciples' journey depends. Thus He first by a threefold revelation of Himself lays down the conditions of their journey ; I am the Way, the Truth, and the Life : and then He points to the conditions and the goal of their journey as alike determined by His ; No one cometh unto the Father save through me.

These last words "through me" bind together
the three heads which have preceded. Christ is not
merely the Way and also the Truth and also the
Life; but He is these all at once. Each office involves the others. The coming to the Father by
Him includes all. His hallowing lordship over
human life demands the full and harmonious co-
operation of its several functions. The prætermission
of any one function is to that extent an abnegation of
Him. The limitation of His supremacy to any one
function, while the others are reserved for the control
of self or of the world without, is to that extent a
rebellion against Him. His discipleship and His
apostolate can be duly executed in any one sphere
only when He is recognised and diligently served as
Lord of all.

But the Lordship of Christ is more than an
issuing of commands for His disciples to obey. His
commandments are part of His own action, and His
own action is the foundation of His disciples' action.
His coming to the Father is the prophecy of their
coming to the Father, and the power by which they
are enabled to come. His coming to the Father
followed the close of His work in human flesh, even
of that work which the Father had given Him to do.
We may have a natural shrinking from using language
of this kind; but it is His own language, constantly
repeated; and it is written for our instruction that we
may know the meaning of our own work and our own

sonship. It abounds in His last prayer: "I glorified
Thee on the earth, finishing the work which Thou
hast given me that I should do; and now glorify me
thou Father, with Thyself with the glory which I had,
before the world was, with Thee." "I am no longer
in the world, and they themselves are in the world,
and I come unto Thee." "And now I come unto
Thee, and these things I speak in the world that they
may have the joy that is mine fulfilled in themselves."
The coming to the Father therefore of which He
speaks as set before them can in no sense be an
escape from sharing His work. It is not a private
felicity, to be bought by neglect of the wider fields of
various activity in the midst of which the lot of all
men is cast, and by concentration upon Himself in
isolation from His kingdom. Its joy is that of the
welcome given to the good and faithful servant
bidden to enter into the joy of His Lord.

Except as denoting the crown of willing and
intelligent discipleship, the words "coming to the
Father" have in this connexion no meaning. They
offer no promise except to those who have loved
and honoured the Son. If the responsibility of
sonship and the subjection to the Son are accepted
grudgingly, still more if they are repudiated, 'coming
to the Father' can be only an object of dread. Sub-
mission to the Son of God as the supreme Way,
Truth, and Life is the test whether the sonship of
men and the fatherhood of God are more than hazy

metaphors to be whispered in moods of pathetic languor.

On the other hand it was necessary for Christ's first disciples in prospect of His departure, and it is necessary for all who in any measure succeed to their discipleship now, that coming to the Father should be distinctly pronounced to be the goal of the journey, the completion of discipleship to the Son. The danger of so cleaving to the Son as to forsake the Father was always close to the Eleven ; and it is of perpetual recurrence. The whole of Christ's own teaching had been directed towards strengthening no less than widening the ancestral faith in the Lord God of Israel. The stronger the affirmation of His own Divine nature, the clearer became His testimony to the Father who sent Him. When the Jews sought to kill Him because He not only loosened the sabbath but also called God His own Father, making Himself equal to God, His answer was, "Verily verily I say to you the Son can of Himself do nothing unless He see the Father doing it ; for what things He doeth these the Son also doeth in like manner: for the Father loveth the Son and sheweth Him all things whatsoever He doeth Himself, and greater works than these shall He shew Him, that ye may marvel." When they murmured because He spoke of having come down out of the heaven, He answered, "No one can come unto me except the Father which sent me draw him :" and again, "It is written in the prophets, 'And they shall be all taught of God:' every one therefore who heareth from the Father and learneth cometh unto me". Yet the nature of the personal devotion to Himself which went on increasing, necessary as it was for the time and the purpose, might well, if it had continued longer in its original shape, have imperilled the faith in the invisible Father. The danger lay not in an increase of faith in Christ but in an adhesion to Him which was not faith, as walking with Him not by faith but by sight. The possibility of the danger lurks in St Philip's request, "Lord, shew us the Father and it sufficeth us": his Lord, he felt, was manifest to him; the Father, he supposed, was not; he had no desire to let go the Father, but while the Lord on earth was known to him by flesh and blood, the God above was becoming to him a shadowy name in contrast. Christ's departure then came at the right season: it was time not only that the personal Guide should Himself become known as the Way, the Truth, and the Life, but that all progress in Him should be seen to conduct to the Father. This had been the original purpose for which the disciples had been drawn to the Son. Coming to Christ had a separate meaning only while Christ was gone out from the Father into the world. To choose it afterwards as a better and dearer privilege than coming to the Father would have been to return perversely to the unripe partial discipleship of the probationary period,—discipleship, that is, to a Christ after the flesh, a Christ not glorified, because either not slain, or else slain only but left hanging on the Cross,—not buried, and not raised from the dead.

Thus the Lord taught His disciples that the long and various journey which was henceforth to constitute the following of Him was not a random wandering but a perpetual progress towards a certain end. The end was nothing less than the Father's immediate presence. While Christ as the One Way, the One Truth, and the One Life took up into Himself the whole universe as related to man, even as it first came into being through Him the Eternal Word, yet He was not Himself the end. Those to whose goings and knowledge and affections He gave at once the master impulse and the ruling standard would be thereby conducted to His Father and their Father, His God and their God. Each step in discipleship to Him would be a step in the perfecting of sonship to God. Of the Word become flesh it was true as it was in the elder time, "As many as received Him, He gave them authority to become children of God."

These considerations may help us to understand how it was that the Lord was not content with saying "Through me shall ye come unto the Father," but shut out all vaguer possibilities by a peremptory negation, "No one cometh unto the Father save

through me". Part of the undefined mistrust with
which we all sometimes shrink from accepting the
declaration in its full rigour arises from a proneness
to paraphrase the words 'cometh unto the Father' by
some loose notion of arriving ultimately at happiness.
Yet they are fixed to their strict sense by the occasion
on which they were used, and by the whole context.
The human coming to the Father derives its character
from the homeward return of Him in whom the Father
was well pleased. Such a return implies of necessity
the mind and spirit of sonship ; and where these have
yet to be formed, discipleship to the Eternal Son has
yet to begin.

On another side the exclusiveness of Christ's
affirmation is inseparable from the nature of the
office which He has been claiming for Himself. Its
effect is simply to fix with absolute certainty the
definiteness and universality of the preceding revelation. It forbids us to understand Christ as saying
no more than, "I am a way, I am truth, I am life."
On the other hand it receives its own interpretation
from the threefold revelation. "Through me" cannot
mean only "by my favour" or "by my intercession":
it cannot bear any sense limited by the conditions
of a single human career: it is coextensive with
the Way, the Truth, and the Life.

Since then these two parts of the Lord's answer
to St Thomas mutually explain each other, the exclusiveness of the second declaration becomes an

assurance that the keys of all worlds with which we
have to do are in the hands of Him who took our
nature and died for our sake. His exclusive mediation means first the unity of all things in Him, and
then the privilege bestowed on us as His brethren
of finding that when we yield ourselves to Him all
things whatsoever that we touch are bearing us onward to God. All things lead to Him ; while through
Him alone can any one come to the Father ; and there
is no way that can be walked in, no truth that can
be known, no life that can be felt and lived, which
is without access to the Supreme Way, the Supreme
Truth, the Supreme Life. We are taught by the
Apostles to believe that there is a Divine purpose in
every outward and inward movement of man and
of all creation. We are taught that the Eternal Word,
He who is in the bosom of the Father, is the expression of that purpose and the accomplishment
of it. We are taught that His Incarnation was the
primary accomplishment of it for mankind, and the
revelation of its full accomplishment hereafter. We
are taught that men, being instructed out of the im-
perishable record of His revelation by the progressive
enlightenment of His Spirit, are able in part to
discern this purpose, and to yield willing service
towards its fulfilment. But then if this teaching be
true, to suppose that any one could come to the
Father except through the Son would involve the
strangest contradiction.

The exclusiveness of Christ is in truth but another name for the absolute universality of His kingdom combined with its absolute unity.

But what is the meaning of this coming to the Father by the Son? Can these theological mysteries be translated into common experience when we close our books and go forth into the open air? It is in the open air that we may best learn what they mean. We know that there is around us what we call the world: we have been told, and we partly believe, that there is above us One whom we call God. We know that at every moment we are acted on by the world: we are told, and we partly believe, that we were created and that we are sustained by God. We know that we cannot stir a finger without ourselves acting on some part of the world: we are told, and we partly believe, that all we do is marked and judged by God. We know that the world is full of objects which attract that which is in us, drawing forth our desires and energies towards them. We are told, and we partly believe, that God claims the direction of our hearts to Him. Our time, our capacity, our mental and bodily force are limited: how are we to apportion them between the world which we hear calling to us from around and from below, and the God whom we suppose to be calling to us from above? Are the two powers entirely at variance, or do they at all coincide in their requirements, and if so, how far?

The most obvious answers to these questions are those which bid us disregard the one power or the other. The readiest expedient of course is to dispense with God, as the most distant and uncertain if not the least substantial power. So we turn to the world and offer it our whole heart. But then the world itself has within it many worlds, and if we are honest with ourselves the old perplexity starts up on a fresh scale. Everywhere we have offered to us a higher world and a lower. The lower world is always the most tangible, obtrusive, alluring. The higher world is always the most impalpable, secluded, severe. We may choose lower world after lower world; but we cannot find satisfaction.

But we might have paused after the first step. Though God be shut out, there still remain affections, duties, philanthropies, arts, knowledges, innumerable works and ways which are not base and which can be pursued with an untroubled conscience. They are often invaded and corrupted by the earthlier powers below with which they cannot dispense; and some of their worst dangers are linked to their greatest necessities; but they can likewise often maintain themselves, though hardly make progress, under the protection of habits and customs and institutions. But they live only as long as they are not called on to give account of themselves. If once they become subjects of free and energetic thought, their stability is sapped. They have no sufficient reason to plead why they should not be banished as God was banished before them.

On the other hand the effort to cleave to God and dispense with the world, though it proceed from the noblest impulse, and often is fruitful of precious results, is condemned to inconsistency from the first. The lowest necessities of human existence are inexorable, [and in the endeavour to sacrifice the world to God,] life is consumed in a vain and impossible effort to hate and despise all the outward and inward works of His hands except the feelings which are directed exclusively towards Himself, and the acts and objects in which such feelings are conventionally expressed; while the deadly power of spiritual evil is in danger of being forgotten. Yet this sacrifice is fruitless as to its intended result, for the God worshipped in wilful forgetfulness of His creatures is a spectral idol, a figment of the human heart or brain.

All lower and imperfect forms of Christian faith are vain attempts to combine the two antagonistic views by arbitrary apportionment of human service between the outward world and God. They can never satisfy a fully awakened conscience or an instructed and unsophisticated reason. They cannot free themselves from an uneasy sense of impotent inconsistency, a consciousness that high purposes are being mutilated and deformed by reluctant acquiescences, and yet that there is no escape except by yet more ignoble compromises.

The only peace which can close this discord is
the peace of the Son of God, His redemption of
the world which came into being through Him, and
of which He is the Life, the Truth, and the Way.
All our primary knowledge of God is through Him,
the true Son of the true Father. All our primary
knowledge of Him, the Son, is through His revelation
in human flesh and blood under the conditions of
earthly life, and through the testimony of those who
had conversed with Him by their bodily senses. All
our thoughts of heavenly things are therefore shaped
out of earthly images. All service rendered to God
is the service of His Son's kingdom, and it is rendered
in and through and to the work which He is ever
carrying on in the world. All elements of our being
within, all objects and forces over which we can
put forth any influence without, are made for His
service, and attain their own special perfection only
when they are turned towards Him. For while all
things in their Divine order lead up to Him, each
separate thing in its own form, function, and life is
contemplated by Him, and His delight and glory is
in all.

To be independent of the world is impossible :
to be independent of God is to lose the life of life.
We enter on the freedom of God's children when we
learn so to use the world that it brings us nearer
God ; and that use of it is its own true and proper
use. The transformation is not without but within,

or at least it begins within. It involves the subjuga-
tion of all lawless desires and covetings, all sloths,
all prides and vanities, all bitternesses and resent-
ments. It consists in the moulding of action and
thought and feeling by the Way, the Truth, and the
Life as set forth in the Gospel, and by experience
read according to that standard. Then the love of
all things high and low is deprived of power to
estrange from God, and becomes an enrichment of
devotion to Him and a means of furthering His
purposes. He is not to be worshipped in emptiness.
The wider and fuller our communion with His works,
the closer and healthier will be our communion with
Him.

It is to the upper room at Jerusalem that we must
return at last if we would receive our Lord's word
in its pure force. None are present there but Himself and His chosen, and they too are soon to be
separated. Every word is personal : abstractions are
far removed. The way to be trodden, about which
St Thomas had asked, is suddenly lifted into personality by identification with the Lord Himself;
and then beneath the Way the Truth, and beneath
the Truth the Life are raised to the same height.
Yet here the personal mode of expression alone
is strictly true; the impersonal names are dilutions of the truth meeting the weakness of human
faculties. But the words, strange to hear from human

lips under any circumstances, must have been ⌐amazing⌐
to the disciples in that hour. The claim seemed to
be made only that the morrow might falsify it. But
the morrow was destined in truth to establish it
for ever by concentrating at once upon it every power
that could destroy. The Way, the Truth, the Life
were to be baptized at once into death, sprinkled with
the blood of the Cross. As the first lesson of the new
discipleship the disciples were to learn that walking in
the Way and knowing the Truth and living in the
Life demand not exemption from self-surrender but
the readiest acceptance of it. All human interests
bore a part in the agony of the Son of Man: all
had to die that they might live.

The chief office of the disciples as apostles, admitted to know the counsel of God as revealed in
His Son, was to work out the purpose directly in
virtue of their knowledge of it, and to provide for
its wider and later working out by transmitting to
others their own testimony and their own authority.
Such also has been the work intended to be performed, and in part actually performed, by the Church
in all ages. But it is a striking characteristic of the
words of the Apostles after the Ascension that they
hold up with equal force the unconscious working
out of God's counsel by evil men. " There were
gathered together of a truth in this city against Thy
holy child Jesus, whom Thou didst anoint, both Herod
and Pontius Pilate with the nations and peoples of

Israel, to do whatsoever things Thy hand and counsel foreordained to come to pass."

The faith and wisdom which they shewed by these and the like tokens were the fruits of the teaching received around the table of the Last Supper, when it had been illumined by the experiences of the following days and weeks. Christ's disciples in all ages are tempted to think that His operation is limited to their own number, and that He is mighty only when they are mighty, weak when they are weak. If then after a time of familiar presence among them He seems to be taking His departure, this is once more no sign that He is abdicating His Lordship, or that obedience and faith in His Lordship are ceasing to be the first condition of sure stability and sure progress for mankind, with new power over a wider field in ways hitherto unseen. He is breaking up an immature discipleship now verging towards a custom only too compatible with faithlessness that He may recreate it on a wider scale, with larger demands on wisdom and devotion, and greater and more various work to do. In so far as He hides Himself as man, it is that He may manifest Himself as God.

*　　*　　*　　*　　*　　*　　*　　*

Once more the hour of the Church's trial in all its forms compels us each and all to see that we too are passing through an hour of trial, and those of us most

whose manhood is now beginning. A future lies in
front which cannot possibly be the same as the past:
but the past is there, fixed and indestructible: we can
no more strip it off than we can strip off body and
soul. Not in vain at the beginning of our personal
past, while the conscious recognition of self was as
yet unborn, were we washed with water and marked
with the cross as members of Christ, children of God,
and heirs of the kingdom of heaven. Not in vain
was our name, the symbol of the personal unity in
which the various elements of our nature are held
together, bestowed solemnly upon us in the Name of
names, the name of the Blessed Trinity. Not in vain
were we pledged to a never ending discipleship to
Christ, and fellowship in the Church of His disciples.
These acts of consecration, being performed upon us
from without, herein faithfully represent the greater
part of our present selves. By inheritance and by
education for the most part we are what we are:
what we have received is the foundation of all that
we can do. Sonship to the Father, discipleship to
the Son, fellowship in the Spirit are upon us. We
can abjure them if we will, but we cannot annihilate
them: we cannot make ourselves as though they had
never existed. Yet neither can they retain their
accustomed form. If we do not choose to go backward, we must go forward. We must labour to
accept them more completely as determining the
purpose of our lives.

We are full of inconsistencies, and so is all around us. But those inconsistencies are the mark of the passage from the lower consistency of unconscious animal life to the higher consistency of spiritual life, preserving and perfecting every element of the animal life yet transforming it by the new creation. To go back now to the lower consistency means to choose chaos, darkness, death. Each noble inconsistency results from some one fragment of discipleship, some accepted task of sonship. Yet we ought never to be satisfied with inconsistency. We must struggle forward towards a rational and effectual unity. The conditions of that unity are, the Gospel tells us, to be found only in Christ the Son of God. We want a principle of conduct, a truth which will satisfy reason, a flow of inward life. We want all these, each for its own sake, and each for the sake of the others: yet for the sake of one we are constantly driven to sacrifice the rest. There is but one perfect unity, and that is in the heavens: yet it came down from the heavens that we might be raised into fellowship with it. Daily taking up the cross and following Jesus the Christ as Lord, daily turning and becoming as little children in the Sonship of the Heavenly Father, are the means by which it is attained. So with all our own inconsistencies and weaknesses and sins we are kept in the One Way, the One Truth, and the One Life ; and each step that we take brings us nearer to the One Father above.

APPENDIX.

NOTES AND ILLUSTRATIONS.

οὗτος ὁ ἀπ᾽ ἀρχῆς, ὁ καινὸς φανείς, καὶ παλαιὸς εὑρεθείς, καὶ πάντοτε νέος ἐν ἁγίων καρδίαις γεννώμενος. οὗτος ὁ ἀεί, cήμερον γἱὸς λογιcθείς, δἰ οὗ πλουτίζεται ἡ ἐκκληcία, καὶ χάρις ἁπλουμένη ἐν ἁγίοις πληθύνεται, παρέχουcα νοῦν, φανεροῦcα μυcτήρια, Διαγγέλλουcα καιρούς, χαίρουcα ἐπὶ πιcτοῖc ἐπιζητοῦcι, Δωρουμένη οἷc ὅρκια πίcτεωc οὐ θραύεται οὐδὲ ὅρια πατέρων παρορίζεται....ἧν χάριν μὴ λυπῶν ἐπιγνώcῃ ἃ λόγος ὁμιλεῖ, δἰ ὧν Βούλεται, ὅτε θέλει.

THIS (THE WORD OF THE FATHER) IS HE WHO WAS FROM THE BEGINNING, WHO APPEARED AS NEW, AND WAS FOUND TO BE OLD, AND IS BORN AT ALL TIMES YOUNG IN THE HEARTS OF THE HOLY. THIS IS HE WHO IS EVERMORE, TO-DAY ACCOUNTED A SON, THROUGH WHOM THE CHURCH IS ENRICHED, AND GRACE SPREADING WIDE IN THE HOLY IS MULTIPLIED, PROVIDING REASON, MANIFESTING MYSTERIES, ANNOUNCING SEASONS, REJOICING OVER THE FAITHFUL WHEN THEY SEEK, BESTOWING ON THEM GIFTS BY WHICH THE SACRED BONDS OF FAITH ARE NOT WEAKENED NOR THE LANDMARKS OF THE FATHERS OVERSTEPPED....WHICH GRACE IF THOU GRIEVE NOT, THOU SHALT LEARN TO KNOW THOSE THINGS WHICH THE WORD DISCOURSES, BY WHAT MEANS HE CHOOSES, AT WHAT TIMES HE WILLS.

ANONYMUS SAEC. II.

APPENDIX.

NOTES AND ILLUSTRATIONS.

ON THE ACQUISITION AND TRANSMISSION OF TRUTH.

Smooth ways of thought are like smooth ways of action: truth is never reached or held fast without friction and grappling.

To move in the direction where movement is easiest is not action or work: all action involves struggle and conquest.

We want not relaxation but bracing and binding: we are all abroad, never at home. We need to live with girded loins and lamps burning, ready instantly to throw ourselves on what is needed. Yet the time is gone by for gaining concentration by narrowness of aim.

We must beware of a slavery of the mind to its own tools, not the less tools that they are part of its furniture and frame.

All processes of logic and method are only mechanism, extending and correcting the inborn mechanism of the eye.   Behind, and apart from all alike is the power of sight.

Vision.

Its three qualities are clearness, completeness, proportion.

Vision is essentially personal and individual, involving selection and interpretation.

No hearsay can be a substitute.   What we have ourselves seen and learned and known is the dominant and the vitalising factor in all real belief.

Yet within the narrowest sphere we have to depend at second hand on the ⌐vision⌐ of others.

And the necessity increases with each expansion of our own range of vision, till personal experience is found to be the merest atom of the vital experience of mankind; and that total experience (itself evidently as yet an imperfect representation of truth, even of truth in relation to man) is needed to be in some degree assimilated if our own view of things is to be even approximately true.   Truth and reality suffer if either factor is allowed to overpower the other. To gain a true view we must take into account all varied forms of contemporary experience, and all the experiences of different ages.   He will best see the whole, and each part in relation to the whole most truly, who has the widest and best proportioned knowledge founded on the experience of others, and at the same time controls all by his own experience. He cannot be too conscious of its pettiness, or of its ultimate claim on his fidelity.

Our sight of things unseen is now 'through a mirror, in a riddle,' much more therefore the thought by which we try to conceive, much more again the speech by which we try to utter our thought. We have to be content with approximations, and also to uphold them as worth having, fragments of substantial truth, enveloped in wrappings of secondary falsehood from which we never can wholly disentangle them, though it is our duty to be always working towards that end. In trying to escape from this need of approximations we necessarily fall into one of the twin forms of what is the same fundamental error, by seeking refuge either in dogmatic authority, or in abandoning the whole sphere of knowledge in which the approximations lie.

It is the special power of poetry that it tells of life, and therewith fuses and unifies all things: thus if merely articulate, it loses its living character; if it contains no truth, the life is felt to be fleeting and can only charm for an hour. The life which is eternal must be identical in substance with truth, truth itself presented under another ordering to another order of perception.

One power of life is to break down barriers and distinctions created for logic. Yet it is never solvent or chaos-producing. It implies for its continuance an infinite diversity of function, though with limited powers of transference. Not exclusive of truth but requiring a subtlety of gradation, a variation in continuity, which transcends the power of the logical or scientific faculty; and of which the higher mathematics alone present an image.

There is a tendency to deny all knowledge not manifestly demanding sympathy. Aesthetic perception is part of sympathy. The highest art is that which most weaves together sympathies of various orders, *i.e.* is in the truest sense sacramental. Universal sympathy and universal knowledge are mutually required. The limitations of the knowledge possible to any man are consequent on the limitations of his sympathy. Knowledge in the narrower sense is the articulation of the sight which accompanies sympathy.

All our knowledge is affected by our personality, and this really makes it knowledge. The naked reflexion of a mirror is not knowledge. Whatever is cognized becomes knowledge only by combination either with other cognitions that we possess or may possess or else by combination with our life or our action.

The vain effort to attain a purely 'objective' or

detached view implies the possibility of emancipation from ancestry or from past and present environment.

Experience and Revelation.

In human science historic fact, unique and individual, is the base: in natural science uniform repetition of likenesses, while each is and must be influenced by the other.

Experience is unsafe only so far as incomplete; false only by false and arbitrary selection out of experience. No line is possible between what has come to men, and their interpretations of what has come to them. Dissect experience into its elements as we may, each element contains both factors. All that has been thought and felt is experience, and all but the most elementary experience has no way of finding expression and record but in images.

To reduce experience to (supposed) primary sensations or to what can supply unchanged the materials for logical processes is to destroy experience.

Experience also gives but specimens, from which we with greater or less certainty infer what has not come within our ken. The words and facts of gospel history and of apostolic history do not the less belong to experience because they have relations to miracle. The problem in respect of them is, are they (supposing them to be truly recorded) most truly interpreted by

the supposition of miraculous antecedents and con-
comitants or not? As historical and literary phenomena they demand to be subjected to historical
and literary criticism. But they do not stand unique
in a crowd of uniformitarian experience. Waiving
miracle, experience itself supplies every grade of
uniqueness, and the uniqueness of gospel miracle is
but a culmination not an isolated presentation.

Reason.

It may be urged that the right or rather duty of
personal verification of truth here maintained is in
effect to set up the authority of reason in matters of
faith. So be it. There can be no surer sign of
decrepitude and decay in faith than a prevalent
narrowness about naming and commending reason,
an unwillingness to allude to its existence except
under wrappings of language which suggest that it
is but a necessary evil. The fear of doing injury to
the unstable by a bolder policy is perversely fallacious.
The faith of ordinary people would be far more clear
and sure if they had been freely instructed in the
responsibilities of reason. Our present cowardice
moreover is of modern growth.

Fear of a truth without can only be cured by
taking it within, or rather accepting it as already
within.

Yet on another ground the wisdom of uplifting

the banner of reason may be justly questioned, namely on account of the incurable ambiguity of the term itself.

Criticism.

Criticism is not dangerous except when, as in so much Christian criticism, it is merely the tool for reaching a result not itself believed on that ground but on the ground of speculative postulates; while such postulates though they may be suggested by a multitude of facts (sc. the irrelevant facts) yet draw their strength rather from the temporary feeling of an age, in other words from a masked authority or tradition, or because an individual mind feels them needed for its own inner repose, and will not be disturbed by new facts.

ON APOLOGETICS.

On the work of an Apologist.

There is an antithesis between preservation of old truth and acquisition of new. It occurs both within the individual and in his relations to ⌈the outer world⌉. At each moment he has his own convictions, the result of his past. Whether obtained by inheritance, or by repudiation of inheritance, or by personal acquisition, in any case they stand over against the present and future processes of his mind. He must start from

them even when he is correcting them. If he cares
for truth and its reception he must be their apologist
and propagator no less than their critic. To detach
himself from them for the purposes of criticism is an
impossibility, and the attempt a delusion.

The analogy holds for his dealings with the truth
of the Church or of society generally. A large part of
his duty to society or to his own special society
consists in the preservation and propagation of truth
already ascertained, no matter from what source and
by what means. It is in danger of being forgotten,
invaded by moral evil, invaded by unconscious en-
croachment and perversion, invaded by deliberate
assault and deliberate unfounded change. If a teacher
of others, he must teach primarily out of ascertained
truth, and he must in some measure deal with current
language and notions, however conscious of their
inadequacy. Yet even without this special responsibility, the duty of preservation is always grave: and
there is the added responsibility attaching to him as
a loyal member of a special society endowed with a
special truth. Yet equally clear is the duty of perpetual correction, perpetual progress. There is a
necessary preservation which is simply apologetic:
the more powerful preservation comes by perilous use
and perilous reform.

The appeal to Credentials.

The most tempting form of simplification is that
which throws the whole burden upon credentials.
This is the contention which finds most favour with
those Christians who prize their belief chiefly as
either dogma or law.

The exclusive appeal to credentials is ultimately
an appeal to external signs of supernatural power
and knowledge in our Lord and the apostles. If
these can be established, they seem to set aside all
necessity for calling in human history, or authority,
or conscience, or reason. Such calling in is manifestly
inconvenient when any particular doctrine assumed
to be Christian is assailed : the task is much easier to
have only to say,—' This rests on the direct authority
of the Lord and the apostles, who are proved to have
had supernatural knowledge.' But supposing the
supernatural power and knowledge proved, what do
they prove beyond themselves?

The appeal to Contents.

The unsatisfactoriness of Christian evidences is
partly owing to the fact that they necessarily endeavour to detach Christianity from the sum of objects
of knowledge and belief.

The Christianity that can be thus presented is

only a part of the whole, and that distorted by its detachment.

Christianity consists of the most central and significant truth concerning the universe, intelligible only in connexion with other truth not obviously Christian, and accepted by many not Christians. If it is assumed as true, the universe can be beheld as subject to a comparatively worthy order which falls to pieces when Christianity is assumed to be a delusion.

All the great speculative questions are insoluble except on some view which gives unity to the universe. The desire of unity may be stigmatised as a mental disease; but the very notion of diseases assumes a kind of unity : and so always the only rational question is What kind of unity ? The unity given by God in Christ alone preserves all things in integrity and unfrustrated, it alone being unity with universal comprehension through subordination : but this it does by a reconstitution, a new creation.

Christianity is not an uniform and monotonous tradition, but to be learned only by successive steps of life.

Two questions arise, whether belief in God ought to be added as a supplement to other beliefs : and whether belief in Christ ought to be added as a supplement to belief in God. Both alike are insoluble. Belief in

Christ is not a supplement to belief in God but the only sure foundation of it. Belief in God is not a supplement to other beliefs, but the only bond of their coherence and trustworthiness.

If the summing up of all things has not already come down to meet us from the heavens, new attempts at partial summings up will rise from the earth like the crests of surging waves, but rise only to fall.

The modern desire is for truth omnigenous, but scattered : it must be built up together before it can furnish food for wisdom and so for conduct : and we shall increasingly find the impossibility of so building without the keystone which the knowledge of God supplies. The light from above here most of all—though in its measure everywhere—must meet the search from below.

Out of Christ all that is behind is dead. We cannot legitimately knit together moment to moment or limb to limb. But in Him the whole dead past becomes alive again : it is part of His body and His life flows through every part.

So also is the dead universe of multitudinous forces or atoms which meet and part and whirl in mad restlessness.

The experience of the Church in all ages concerning life and concerning the relation of life to
Christ, has had the same twofold character as the
parallel experience concerning the Truth and the
Way. From the earliest times till now a bright and
fruitful life has been entering into men from their
Divine Head through devotion to His Person. From
the earliest times till now the life descending from
Christ has often been defiled with corruption, often
been stricken with barrenness; it has often itself well-
nigh succumbed to foes without or languors within; and
the deepest of all causes of failure has been imperfect
apprehension of the full truth contained in the word
spoken to St Thomas. Christians have looked up to
Christ as life-giving and as life; in so far as they
have not known Him as ' The Life,' they have fatally
misread themselves and mankind and the world, and
His work in and for all.

The history of the Church, if it could ever be truly
written, would be the most composite of all histories,
since it would have to set forth the progress of every
element of humanity since its invisible Head was
revealed.

The amplest knowledge of human acts, or even
human beliefs, without some corresponding knowledge of the human vicissitudes of the life beneath,
could never supply an answer to the ancient
question, which insistently asks itself to-day, What
new thing Christ brought into the world?

In the times when Christianity owed nothing to custom and tradition, and when all the ways of ordinary society tended to draw men away from it, what drew them to it and held them to it despite all persecution was the power of its life. Naturally this was the element which could give least account of itself. Many were drawn by the testimony of the moral power of Christianity, a few by the satisfaction which it gave to reason. But life calling to life was the one victorious power which mastered men and women of all conditions and of all grades of culture.

If it be urged that this defence of Christianity, as being dependent on its own character and especially on the widest view of the province of religion, is inapplicable to most current forms of Christianity, the plea must be acknowledged as true. By their limitation of its claims, and also by their manner of conceiving some of the Christian doctrines (partly owing to the limitation, partly for other reasons), they fail to be covered by what is here said. Nay, were Christianity such as it is represented in them, I could not accept it myself. Part only of its evidence would remain valid, and there would be more than a mere diminution in its amount : there would be insuperable contradiction between (supposed) actual Christian doctrine and what I could not but believe.

Most of the distortions and contradictions which render some of the best known forms of Christianity incredible as wholes are corollaries from a view of God's counsels towards mankind and the universe which transposes the primary end and the secondary means. Finite as we are, our knowledge of God's purposes, especially in our present unripened state, can be only partial and approximative: the glory of God, which stands in Scripture as the furthest goal in our horizon, is richly significant indeed, but yet transcends all conceptions in which finite things are included. But still it makes all the difference whether our view of God's purposes does or does not invert them within the range which it is at all able to cover. Is it the true sense of Scripture that recompense of human deeds, good or evil, and not the quality of the deeds or the doer, is the prime motive of Divine dealings with mankind? If so, then human morality is better than that which is called Divine. Yet this is the latent premiss in the ordinary conception of salvation.

It is impossible to accept the universal authority of religion while it involves conceptions which poison and unrealize life; and equally impossible to accept a partial authority for religion, though its specialities must be partial by the nature of the case. Its extension to universality must go hand in hand with its enrichment and restoration out of false negativity. The process is easily misrepresented as a hollow sanctifying of the crude or unregenerated world (which hollow sanctifying is indeed a true and most serious peril on one side). Nevertheless religion can rule only in proportion as it becomes worthy to rule, and the due honour which it learns to pay to all departments of human action in their several places is on one side the measure of its worthiness.

Ethical impossibilities.

I. The assumed premiss that recompense of human deeds (not the quality of the deeds or the doer) is the prime motive of Divine dealings with mankind. (Interchange of Law and Gospel.)

II. That even correction (to say nothing of requital) of evil is the starting point of God's dealings with man rather than good. (Creation)(Fall.)

III. (Corollary of I.) that this present life is to be disparaged, and made a mere antecedent to the future, not worthy of intrinsic dignity and cultivation. (Impossibility of keeping this view consistently. Secularism preferable to its consistent adoption.) On the other hand there is a true subordination of the present to the future.

In affecting to defend Christianity are you not replacing Christianity as it is by a personal product of your own ?

Ans. There is no 'Christianity as it is,' but a multitude of Christianities each of which covers a small part of what is believed in the nineteenth century, while this as a whole excludes much that has been believed in past centuries, and the sum of the whole covers but a part of the contents of the Bible. It is true that certain modifications of doctrine have been much more widely current in different ages, and in different places in the same age, than others; but, the moment we study the greater theologians who have done more than reflect or even systematise current beliefs, we find the harmony broken, and we often find also these isolated but not isolating voices to reflect the inarticulate feelings of the simply devout who are not theologians and do not think it necessary to repeat the phrases of their friends or teachers.

Hence the vital need of the study of the history of doctrine.

Linear progress means often the neglect of such elements as are not taken up for development.

But no possible modification can be accepted as Christianity which contradicts the broad testimony of Scripture, and requires the rewriting of its most distinctive passages.

Progress in theology does not consist in mutilation but in purification. It is not the great facts or ideas that are false, but the way in which they are conceived, especially as to the conditions of their external manifestation (false philosophy wrongly supposed to be theology). And so in what concerns the relation of things Divine to men, error lies mainly in attempts to render wholly explicable what is but partly apprehensible : and especially in the use of images drawn from lower rather than from higher human relations and transactions.

Nor does progress consist in being less ecclesiastical.

(1) In the past. Partly what is corrupt and mischievous has proceeded from the Church as such only in the same way as what was sound and beneficial came from the Church as such, both being likely under an unchurchly state of things to have been much less. Partly, much of what is evil arises from the usurpation of the office of the Church by the individual and by mere public opinion &c.

(2) In the future. The great defect of present Christianity is its loss of a social character, in other words its unchurchliness. Where powers and institutions survive, or even dominate, they have ceased to hold their proper place as organs of a living body, breathed into by a Divine Spirit.

The Materialist Controversy.

Two ultimate positions, not proved, but likely to be true.

(1) In the past—Man with his whole mental and spiritual nature derived through various steps from

lower beings having no such nature, and those probably in turn from inorganic bodies.

(2) In the present—Man's whole mental and spiritual nature is conditioned by his physical nature and its pathological states, no mental or spiritual movement taking place without a concomitant physical movement.

These two positive affirmations leave untouched the invisible conditions without which the smallest change 'continuous' or 'discontinuous,' cannot be accounted for, and therefore the invisible Power from which these conditions proceed, and from whom other worlds inaccessible to our present faculties with their conditions may proceed.

They simply affirm two weighty truths about one class of facts, implying by their want of self-sufficiency the existence of other classes of facts, which we may call physical if we please: but affording no evidence positive or negative as to the existence of yet other facts ⌜of Divine agency⌝ underlying these.

They contribute nothing to the proof or disproof of God, merely extending to the whole range of His working within our known world that which every one believes to be true as to a greater or less part of His working.

They contribute nothing to the proof or disproof of immortality.

LIFE.

Life and death are perhaps the most pregnant of images. Yet they are used so manifoldly that their strictest sense is hard to seize.

Even as to physical life various accidents determine the use. With their use in imagery the multiplication of sense becomes still greater.

Thus the mere fact of using the words together leads to opposing them to each other as in some sense equals, a sense not unknown in the Bible. But if we desire to seize the force of either in cardinal passages of the N. T. we must strip off all secondary and derivative associations, and all deductions from speculative theory, and go back to the most naked physical facts of primitive experience.

The true primary contrast is one of observation, not of reflexion.

Life is simply the difference between a body and a corpse ; between a corpse grown cold yet without outward sign of decay, and the same body as it would be seen in a momentary gaze before the change.

The sense arrived at here derives its force from the combination and contrast of like and unlike. It rests on the assumed and manifest resemblance of the dead form to the living form, and even on the completeness of the resemblance.

The most exact memory of shape and line can find no difference.

The difference is invisible, but the invisible difference cannot be forgotten.

It strikes the dullest savage as much as ourselves. To him it is perhaps the clearest and strongest suggestion of the unseen. He knows that the body can eat and move and feel and see or hear and speak, and that the corpse can do none of these things. He is far perhaps from any such wide conception as 'cause' or 'power' but the force of the facts is all the greater. The one form can be made to arise and eat and move and see and feel and speak, or if now asleep it can be waked and then it can be made to do these things. The other cannot : if it is asleep, it is, with a sleep beyond waking. The one form has somehow associated with it something that the other has not, and that something is life.

Decay and dissolution may enter as accessories into the notion of death but only remotely, only perhaps as the movements which the corpse can and will take up if it be not embalmed, but the main feeling is of the absence of what was there before or what is now in some similar form.

Here is half of the true notion of an idol to the worshipper of Jehovah (the other half is its falsehood). Its deadness is a much more positive thing, than that which belongs to a fragment of rock or the trunk of a tree.

It draws its deadness from its semblance of life.

It is the mere semblance of a man or other creature, not even the reality of a bull or an eagle.

It is a corpse-god, not a living God.

This primitive mode of conceiving natural life is the foundation of the secondary sense which comes at a later time of religious reflexion.

After the idea of walking in righteous ways or ' ways of the Lord ' has long prevailed, the thoughts turn inward and the communion with God rises to a higher level.

Then a difference is felt to exist among men analogous to that which distinguishes a body from a corpse. Among those who are engaged in every pursuit of life there is felt to be something in some which is not in others. The outward fashion of the doings differs little or not at all. All are pursuing the same occupations, meet with the same accidents of life and are subject to the same cycle of change. Yet the psalmist or wise man or prophet whose heart has been in the presence of God feels that the common busy life of many is in itself as the state of a corpse in contrast with the state of others not outwardly different but who have learnt to look up to God.

In these last there is a second life, a life within and above that universal life which they share with all that breathe, a life exempt from being dried up, for it flows from an ever-living fountain in the heavens.

It was apparently this thought of life that gave rise to the early foreshadowings of personal immortality.

Two characteristics helped to this result.

(1) The life was marked by its power of surviving all shocks and wastings that destroyed the other forms of life, and this although it was ⌐doubly⌐ invisible. Why then should it not survive the last shock of all?

(2) It was sustained by its communion with God, and the fountain in Him was certainly unaffected by human vicissitudes. He lived on from lifetime to lifetime, from generation to generation. Why then should not the streams fed from that fountain be equally free from a destiny of exhaustion?

All life is (1) derived from life, (2) requires sustenance, (3) maintains an unity of different functions, (4) is generative of life.

The highest point of the lower life, 'sensibility,' gives birth equally to thought and to feeling, both usually instinctive but capable of becoming individual and immediate.

Feeling is shaped by appetites and impulses, individual or social, and so gives rise to associated

στοργαί. These στοργαί remain isolated, limited, and
fugitive, always subserving some end of conser-
vation or propagation, and nothing beyond.

When the separate mental and affective actions
come into combination, the στοργαί become tinged
with affections, and the instincts with reason. Then
first there is a conscious self to be indulged or
sacrificed. The passage from the partial human
affections to the generalized affections towards God
or gods is obscure but probably never purely
affective or purely rational.

Life is the power of performing function. It is
the discharge of function that converts labour into
work. So that the fulness of life implies fulness of
function; and life becomes varied with variety of
function.

Life is that which at once reveals dependence on
the medium and is itself most central and centripetal.
But the greater its inner intensity the more can it
draw and subdue to itself the widest medium.

The impulse from which all action proceeds belongs to the region of feeling and emotion.

It may come from one or more appetites of the
individual body or mind, or from complex desires
made up of them but all having self as their object.

It may come from affections directed towards
persons.

But till it is directed towards God, there is no power which can harmonize these different impulses with each other or with the sense of right or the sense of wisdom which stands outside them all. Only when all three meet in one (He who is the Way is the Truth, and He who is the Truth is the Life) can we escape making endless disorder.

'Way' and 'Truth' obviously need external objects: 'Life' because inward seems self-contained, but is not so really. The lower life of man feeds on yet lower life partly, partly on life like itself, the response to itself; and the failure of response is deadening. The life of affection feeds on affection : the life of religion on the sense of God's love and care.

All life in the higher sense depends on some fellowship, an isolated life is a contradiction in terms. Fellowship is to the higher life what food is to the natural life—without it every power flags and at last perishes. The spirit feeds on a person " Except ye eat the flesh etc." (Eucharist and Marriage.)

Self-containment is abnegation of life. Life is only found by being lost.

Life involves multiplicity and energy of relation. Absoluteness is death.

Suffering is proportional to life. Those who have most life suffer most, as they have also most power to resist and overcome suffering.

The personal thirst for enjoyment is always barren except as the awakenment to the consciousness of powers possessed.

Communion is the law of all. The life which strives to be independent degenerates towards lapse into its lower elements.

But also the 'walking' which strives to be independent (self-will) is the same ; and so is self-chosen belief.

I. Early sense of freedom, lost in manhood, is restored in the new freedom of the Way.

II. Early sense of Truth is lost in manhood either through indifference to it, or through devotion to the substitutes furnished either by our own past imperfect ascertainment of truth, or by what a tradition or other external authority dictates to us as truth. Thought is the active reception of truth.

III. Early sense of Life is lost in manhood. Originally it is neither selfish nor unselfish, it joins the self to what is around. It branches off into self-regarding passions, but thereby loses its own livingness. When it is lost, some or all of these passions survive, robbed of their naturalness and instinctiveness and become settled pursuits of selfishness. The new life comes by the impregnation of the original life with eternity (itself not the ghastly spectre of endless duration). This eternal life in one sense is religion (i.e. emotive religion), in another sense the base and

13—2

root of religion in the fullest sense, including the spheres of the Way and the Truth; and in like manner the Word is the Eternal Life.

The life in God is life in Christ and this sustained by all other affections and emotions and forms of life; so that he who loves nothing else but God destroys the possibility of loving God. And conversely, what gives all partial affections an enduring and ennobling character lifting them from the natural life into the eternal life, is the love of God, in which they meet. Left to themselves they fall back into open or disguised selfishness. The sense of right above them may save them much; but in itself it is too alien: only the love of Him who is the Lord of our life and the way of our life is itself at once a life of higher power and an effectual control.

Christ's relations as the Life to all human emotion.

The limitations of fact were such as were inevitable: to exhaust all experience was impossible. But, as containing all human potentialities, however unexercised, He came into contact with all through the plenitude of prophetic sympathy; of which we may form some conception in the sympathetic anticipations of artists and poets.

If evil is negative (not mere absence) or disproportion or displacement, then a participation in the pure roots of all human impulse must be compatible with perfect sinlessness.

THE WAY.

Ethics and ' the Way.'

The belief in 'ways' belongs to common and universal life, and could not be wanting to heathens. All their morals were attempts to unify and exalt ' ways,' destroying the multitudinous tyranny of impulse and pleasures. Thus they had been working upwards towards a Way, and yet had broken off. Consider for instance the Stoic theory of the Cosmos.

Think on the other hand how the Caesar was stepping into the place of the Way, the Truth, and the Life.

No summing up of all the virtues will lead to the kingdom of God.

All virtues imply relations, and all relations imply a hierarchy of functions.

No one is ever made happy or virtuous by what he receives merely, whether it be knowledge or pleasure or any other outward good : what he is in himself and what his work is in relation to the surrounding world of men and things determine for him whether things good in themselves shall be to him food or poison.

Life sought apart from connexion with a Divine
life sinks into pursuit of pleasure. It becomes incoherent and atomic, a mere multitude of rapturous
moments.

The purpose to be aimed at is that every thing in
man may uplift that which is a little lower than itself, as it is itself uplifted from above. There are
many aboves, and the heavenly above can be retained only by recognition and use of the lower
aboves.

Affection begins in duty and is perfected in duty.

Affection without knowledge is a mere blind adhesion, which debases, not exalts, our personality,
and is always prone to fall back into a barren and
enervating luxury of the senses and physical constitution.

Love perishes without an accompanying sense of
duty to visible and invisible Lords.

The theologies which have sundered God's righteousness from His love have done equal wrong to both.

The rapture of separate moments is only a not
yet extinguished spark from a fire which once was
continuous and might have been continuous still.

'Conduct' becomes ultimately merely negative.
It dispenses with an ideal for the individual and
leaves mankind to drift aimless. The animal needs
no aim: he has to feed, propagate, play: if more,
only as means to these ends. But all that makes up
humanity is above these things, and is unintelligible

without some comprehensive end. "The greatest happiness etc." is so far better than a negative morality that it is in a manner comprehensive and looks beyond self: but it only adds together the repetitions of the individual problem which has already failed; and it makes that an end which even for the animal as seen from without (as we can see it) is but a means, though it may be all that he is conscious of.

If within a subjection to a Way and a Truth there were an independence of personality and affections and desires, discipleship would destroy instead of creating unity.

For all true unity is from within: the more coherent the purpose and passion of our lives, the better our actions and thoughts will agree with them, and with each other.

But there is only one real semblance of unity except the unity which is through Christ with God, and that is the unity of self; the most perfect coherence outside the Christian faith is that of him who deliberately arranges his life so that the world shall revolve round himself as its central sun.

He cannot escape arbitrariness of choice in himself between pleasure, or gain, or pride, or power, or he may make a mixture of pleasure and pride and call it self-cultivation but he must let much die for the sake of the rest.

It is a vain dream that the bare notion of the good of mankind will make an unity. Whoever takes it up is blessed by it, though he lays himself open to endless self-deceits : but he succeeds in proportion to the partiality of his aims. He must fail when he tries to be comprehensive.

Christ the Way.

The antithesis ' I ' and ' the Way ' is the pregnant paradox which knits existence together. On the one hand devotion to a person, human or divine, seems in our best moments the all in all of life. Yet it fades and becomes an unreality or a disease when it is not translated into wide and diffusive operation: conversely all worlds of operation fatigue and desolate and come to vanity. In our finiteness we are driven to oscillate between the person and the world, whatever world it may be. But Christ's word exhibits them as meeting in Him. He, the most personal of persons, is also the dominating centre of every world. Most of all is this true of Him as the Way, apparently the most impersonal of all conceptions.

See in Him the world and humanity as they are in God's sight, the embodiment of the invisible kingdom of which the visible world is the garment. See Him as the whole, not the single part which each one of us is; and it must transform our conceptions.

The Way is not the noble phrensy of a solitary

passionate philanthropist but the secret power by
which every higher step in the scale of being is won
and maintained.

Each sufferer and believer whose experience is
recorded in the Psalter was a part of Christ, a fraction
of the Way.

The word of Christ leads to Christ the Word, as
His footsteps along the way lead to Him as the Way.

The Way involves the double office of Christ as
doing for us what we cannot do, and as the power in
which we do all things, and it makes our work, with
all its imperfection, coextensive with His. Whatever
work He performs for us we have in union with Him
to do for ourselves, and for the world. Salvation (the
supreme name including all Christ's work) is a thing
given us, but to be worked out by ourselves, as a
mine or a field.

The necessities of the present and the ideals of
the future are both related to the past. An ideal
shaped by present necessity alone is always untrue to
permanent relations. An attempt to meet present
necessities shaped only by an ideal is always untrue
to fact and baseless. The past is at once the cause
of the present and the womb of the possibilities of
the future.

Christ's bequest to the Apostles is a continuance of
His own office as the Way: the head of the Way in
the heavens is represented by the body of the Way
on earth.

"As my Father hath sent Me, so send I you."
The prerogative thus asserted for the Church is
dependent on its continuity with Him : so far as the
Church enters on a separate way it dissevers itself
from Him and His authority : but it can never reach
concordance with Him through assimilation to the
region through which it moves, through becoming
itself a wilderness, instead of making known that that
region is His possession, to be reclaimed and subdued
for Him by virtue of the Way which runs through it.

The prerogatives of the Church involve no neglect
of the world, no contempt, or indifference.   They are
the one way by which the world can be finally and
permanently affected.   All other good agencies sub-
serve temporary ends : their permanent work comes
only when their relation to the Church is fixed.

Discipleship.

Discipleship (with the Twelve) in its first or
probationary stage, as to One walking among them a
man amongst men, always came near to simple
personal adhesion, dispensing with the use of their
own faculties within and media without, though Christ
was always training them to the use of the one and
the other.

The new stage of discipleship was reached first by
the withdrawal of the bodily presence. Hence forward

if discipleship was persevered in, it could only be faith and obedience.

Discipleship is nothing and means nothing except as the response to a pre-existent and actual lordship, not right to lordship merely, but exercised lordship.

Discipleship begins in obedience, and it ends in obedience, therefore we find it hard to accept: we wish to be mere receivers of good things, and therefore we like to think of Him only as the purveyor of good things.

Yet though we speak of gifts, we take them as rights, we do not like the idea of a giver, and of thanksgiving, because it empties us of ourselves. And so the lowest gifts become the type of all gifts, and even the love of God becomes the pleasure of giving pleasure.

We all want to reverse "Ye have not chosen Me". If we care to have Him for a King, yet it must be as a King of our own making, though He (Jn. vi. 15) "withdrew again into the mountain Himself alone".

Sonship is the true yoke of mankind. All civilization is the yoking of man, and the vicissitudes of history arise out of the trial of various yokes, and the abuse of them by lawless and unyoked power, the rebellions against their misuse involving also rebellion against yokes as such. We have need of Law *and* Gospel. Better Law only than no yoke, and the Gospel is no Gospel if it does not both presuppose and include Law.

The foundations of mental and spiritual health
are obedience, reverence, loyalty, gratitude, in short,
those inward attitudes of thought and emotion which
become beings who are subjects and receivers, and
which are the personal expression of our true
relations to God and men alike. When they are
wanting, morality has ceased to be more than a more
or less slowly dying custom and tradition, sustained
by factitious terrors upheld for the sake of public
convenience.

The ' Citizenship.'

The discipleship in an existing πολίτευμα was a
proper education for disciples who were to constitute
and then to rule a πολίτευμα : their endurance of the
external authorities served a Divine purpose.

For the education of the disciples as belonging to
a πολίτευμα fitted them for seeing the same character
in the faith. Hence the transforming effect of the
Church on the kingdoms of the world. Christians
were instructed to use the temporary pædagogic laws
—experimental, as πρὸς σκληροκαρδίαν—cheerfully
and willingly, as parts of the providential scheme by
which the perfect πολίτευμα may be prepared.

Exampleship.

' Exampleship' is either a fanaticism or a delusion.
St Francis on the one hand ; on the other the affec-
tation of imitating Christ while all actions remain

unchanged. As the Way He is meant to transform us : but the transformation is not into the fashion of Jesus of Nazareth, but into a fashion shaped out of our own materials.

It was not as an Example but as a Master that Christ spell-bound the Apostles.

THE WORDS OF CHRIST.

The Lord held the disciples fast to Himself by a triple attachment, the bond of guidance, the bond of teaching, the bond of life. Each of these bonds was wrought by His words.

The power of the Life that dwelt in Christ comes forth in His words. There are hardly any precepts among them, nothing could be less like the edicts of a law-giver. Almost all are calm affirmations of truth, often sounding like repetition and like vagueness. Yet while the terms elude all efforts at definition the sense of each as a whole is seen to be unutterably precise as we study it.

He speaks often of His own words, summing them up at times into the word or declaration, of which they are all parts, and to which they all contribute.

Their authority He refers to God " the words that I speak unto you, I speak not from myself" (Jn. xiv. 10); and they are the immediate agents of His operation.

His acts are a teaching concerning life, His words pierce to the centre of life and call forth life. So in His prayer He declares " the words which Thou gavest...I have given (not simply spoken but given) to them" (Jn. xvii. 8).

These very words had to be withdrawn, the very vehicle through which all the life had come. The stored-up words were then to be the means of reaching beyond the one word or declaration to the Lord Himself as the Life. This alone could enable them to trust to Him fully as the Truth and the Life.

" Thou hast the words of eternal life." The first impression was not so much of truth as of life or rather of truth merged in life, the two being undistinguishable. But conversely the disciples' expectation of life in Christ, so far as it was felt within (and life cannot be recognized except from within) was through His words: not His mere λαλία, but Himself speaking : written or repeated words have a power, so has a voiceless presence ; but the power of powers among men is when both are combined in the living speaker, who is also a doer, when the pent-up life breaks forth into utterance and becomes articulate, while yet the articulate words are full of the power of the unspoken which remains behind, half intelligible, half not.

The ῥήματα ζωῆς were not declarations much less promises of eternal life. They were vehicles of it. As they entered into the disciples, eternal life entered

in with them. Their operation was on the one hand
that of life, and on the other of life eternal, the
life found in communion with God. Every energy
was quickened, and was turned towards God in the
quickening.

But further His ῥήματα were so completely parts
and utterances of Himself, that they had no meaning
as abstract statements of truth uttered by Him as a
Divine organ or prophet. Take away Himself as the
primary (though not the ultimate) subject of every
statement, and they all fall to pieces. Take away
their cohesion with His acts and His whole known
person and presence, and they lose their power. The
disciples did well to gather from them that He was
the Holy One of God, the chosen and heavenly means
by which God imparts not guidance only, or knowledge only, but the Life that is above.

THE EXCLUSIVENESS OF CHRIST'S CLAIM.

Exclusiveness is the outward expression of unity
combined with universality, the refuge against the
Gods many and Lords many who throng around our
path. We cannot escape doing homage and obedience : the more we rebel, the more abject is our
servitude. But Christ leading to the Father in the
light of the Spirit brings us into the one service
which is in harmony with all the laws of the world
and which breaks the yoke of every other service.

We want to be independent of God, and so fall back into helpless dependence on the world.

If Christ were the chief deity of a pantheon, His exclusive place in the Divine economy would be a robbery of mankind, an arbitrary limitation on opportunities they might have possessed. But the many Gods of a Pantheon are of necessity all the work of men's hearts and brains, whether they be the work of men's hands or not. "They that make them are like unto them, and so are all they that put their trust in them." They are thrust forth out of the earth, and to the earth they fall back again by an inexorable fate. They have no power to carry their worshippers into the presence of the Father who is in the heavens, and they are no less powerless to confer any lasting dominion over the earth.

Christ is the deliverance from idolatry, because we cannot choose but give devotion to near things (to do otherwise we must strip ourselves to an abstract nakedness), and if we give devotion to God also, we fall of necessity into a dualism, which we escape only by making devotion to Him unreal. We choose the near, because we cannot attach ourselves to the distant. But Christ in His fulness brings the distant near and carries the near into the presence of God. In Him each near thing finds a place as the recipient of an immediate and relative devotion, and without the preparation and conduction of such devotion the supreme devotion to God becomes empty and unintelligible.

What we know of the Divine purpose, and what we know of the Father as welcoming His children to His presence not only all hangs alike on the Gospel, but is all part of the same truth.

In a confused way we can cling to the Father without acknowledging the Son: but it is only by abjuring our own sonship: we call ourselves children in tender and pathetic words: but we shrink from sonship as claimed by Christ (Jn. v. 19 f.).

The 'coming to the Father' includes and swallows up the thought of forgiveness in acceptance, acceptance in love. All points to this ideal; but how is it possible if there be no Incarnate Son? There are powers and causes around us, but these, if enduring, are impersonal, the only powers to which we can cleave are those which swiftest vanish, and seem the merest flashes of concurring chances.

Hence in *knowledge* there is no coming without Him, yet not in this only, but in guidance, and in life.

Mediation seems unreal, approached from the side of doctrine, yet it is the summing up of experience in all highest human relations.

It involves no opposition to immediateness of approach. It is the condition of it. It interposes no metaphysical limits or courtly barriers or legality of unforgivingness, but both separation and nearness dissolve into unreality without Him in whom we have 'the access,' and the culmination of all is the atonement (the removal of the most fatal

barrier, whether within ourselves or without), which
seems so incredible while approached singly, rather
than as the perfection of the sacrificing mediation.

The fatal opposition of a monadic soul and a
monadic God is the inevitable result of rejecting mediation : we are driven to strive after an imaginary purity
which reaches perfection only in annihilation.

The word 'Mediator' as applied to Christ theo-
logically has less and less application the more we
study the N.T. (only 1 Tim. ii. 5): but so much
more is the idea of His mediation found to be
universal, and to prevail in it everywhere.

ATONEMENT.

Reconciliation or atonement is one aspect of redemption, and redemption one aspect of resurrection,
and resurrection one aspect of life.   Till the whole is
unrolled, the most comprehensive idea remains empty :
the higher must never be interpreted by the lower,
but the lower by the higher : otherwise in theology
itself we fall into the same vicious method which in
physics leads legitimately to the denial of God.

Sin is a breach in life because it is a separation
between the derivative life and its source : the atonement is the closing up of this breach, and so the
restoration of life.

"No man cometh etc." lays down the condition of

fulfilling "Except ye be converted", while assuming this and not any happiness to be the true aim for men. The salvation of the rational creation consists in the carrying out of this intention, however far the greater part may seem to be from ever having dreamed of it as a possible object of pursuit. But powers above them are· at work as well as powers within them: the stiffest neck has to be bowed and the hardest heart broken.

Salvation only by Christ is a true deduction, but only when salvation is biblically interpreted, viz. as the perfecting of human natures into the mind and form of Sonship in and through the Son.

In loving His children who know Him not, God regards their dormant capacity and works to awake it. Can that be (strictly speaking) loved which has no capacity of response?

The coming to the Father answers to the drawing by Him: compare "I if I be lifted up will draw" (no power to draw except as lifted up) with "No man can come unto Me except the Father draw him." This personal motion belongs to all three regions: and it is a motion of us to God, not of God to us.

'Coming to the Father' may be explained by 'the Prodigal Son.' Departure in a sense from the Father is perhaps a necessity of growth, though not as arising from a desire of a separate portion of goods; but the return to the Father expresses the true relation : even as the son who is always with the father may become unfilial. The 'coming up' (ἄνοδος) to Jerusalem at stated times was a type, a figure of true worshipping: cf. Jn. iv. 21 ff.

Note the correlation of coming to the Father by the Way and coming to the fold of the sheep by the Door.

'Working out' the righteousness and forgiveness of God, and 'revealing' are the same. Revelation and Redemption are always hand in hand; the Revelation is the means by which the Redemption accomplished once for all is made effectual through knowledge.

"This is the Heir: come let us slay Him and the inheritance shall be ours": the inheritance *was* theirs and in slaying the Heir they cast themselves out of it.

COMMUNION.

Communion is permanent, yet needs times of revival.

Prayer is progressive and variable, drawing from the heavenly store.

Our felt wants are of necessity the starting-point of our converse with God. Yet, till we have some joyful apprehension of that in Him which is above and beyond any wants that we have yet felt, it is not really converse with the true and perfect God but with a self-made idol. It is precisely the sense that we are drawing but a few drops from an inexhaustible fountain that keeps faith progressive and makes it not a luxury but an energy.

All Christian life is sacramental. Not alone in our highest act of Communion are we partaking of heavenly powers through earthly signs and vehicles. This neglected faith may be revived through increased sympathy with the earth derived from fuller knowledge, through the fearless love of all things.

All things are given by the ungrudging God ; freely and unreservedly given : "*with* Him freely give all things": not after Him or in addition to Him or as less than Him, but with Him. The gift of Him is that which makes all other gifts true and effectual gifts.

Whatever food the nations enjoy beyond the husks of the swine consists of crumbs from the Master's bread, which was made for His children though they know it not. At last they sit at the table as children in His fatherly presence, and eat their portion with thankfulness, finding there the assurance of His love, and strength to do His work.

The Eucharist is on the one side the ⌐perfection⌐ of the sustenance of life in personal communion, on the other a use of the products of the earth as instruments of communion, implying the necessity of

14—3

taking the whole nature into communion if it is to be real, the symbols of creation and of the Lord's body in one.

The life of the disciples with Christ was exchanged for a life in Christ : they abode as branches in the Vine of which His Father is the Husbandman. The Bread of the Last Supper took for them the place of the Body through which they had first learnt to converse with a living Lord. The Wine of the Last Supper took for them the place of the Blood in which His life had dwelt. In that feast of blessing and thanksgiving, that joyful participation of accepted sacrifice, no life was found too earthly to be offered on the altar of the Cross, or to become a means of human fellowship and Divine Communion.

The Oblation preserved the connexion of life. The fictitious and constructive offering up of a phantom body and phantom blood is a degradation of the Holy Communion to the unreal mimicry of a sacrifice, which if real would now be heathenish.

It is the nemesis of destroying the relation between earthly elements and the heavenly life.

THE DOCTRINE OF THE LOGOS.

The Word was early perceived by that part of the Church which most fully comprehended the completeness of revelation and of redemption. There was danger on that side, the danger of the Truth becoming no more than a philosophy, and the faith in the Son which was needed to sustain the faith in the Word was in the end substituted for it.

But the old faith in the Word must be revived if the Creed is to stand, if Christianity is to be a knowledge. It was the definiteness and personality given to the Word by its identification with the Son, that differenced it from previous doctrines of a word or words: and now fifteen centuries have so firmly fixed the idea of Sonship that there can be no risk that the Church itself should ever merge Him in the Word.

Truth at the last is the word or speech of God.

The truth of Christ may at last restore the lost faith in truth.

GOD AND THE WORLD.

When man sinks into the world, God sinks into it too.

God is sacrificed to the world when His holy Name is added on to the mixed and confused world as it is; when diseases and distortions and inversions and foulnesses are treated as parts of the creation which He pronounced good; and when we are supposed to be equally well-pleasing in His sight whether we are ruled by our own desires from within or the ways and tendencies of men and things from without, or whether we endeavour to bring ourselves and the world about us into conformity with His holy Law.

St John and St Paul are the great bulwarks against a negative Pantheism by the solid personality which they uphold: but it rests no less on their positive Pantheism.

It is vain to uphold either

(1) a merely humanitarian theology: all study of nature dissolves it: an enlarged study of and care for humanity dissolves it hardly less:—or

(2) on the other hand a merely pantheistic theology in combination with a humanitarian morality or anthropology. Both the Pantheistic and the Humanitarian factors are needed in theology and in morality alike, and for the union of both.

No evidences of the supermundane God have any power if we fail to discern the radiations of transmitted and derivative deity as the luminous and vital tissue of finite things.

A twofold veil has been withdrawn from before our eyes: the world has been discovered to us and God has been discovered to us. Neither can now be relinquished: it is a vain dream: account has to be taken of them in all things. Shut them out of self and self vanishes. Shut out either and it returns disguised and falsified. There is no safety but in the full accepting of both in open daylight.

God and the world are believed by their partisans to be enemies, because undoubtedly each can supplant the other up to a certain point.

There is nothing beneath God which cannot be so pursued as to injure His service.

God can be so worshipped in the semblance of devotion as to destroy all interest in the things and persons which surround us, or to make all devotion to them an acknowledged inconsistency, a necessary but lamentable sinfulness.

Yet neither can really be loved without the other. Self is the one rival of both, which takes advantage of all exclusive devotion to either.

Yet the truth is unwelcome, because it demands conversion as little children and refuses to accept current maxims of society as having the slightest validity.

The passage from the one state to the other gives rise to inconsistencies and inequalities, to a time of conflict, which can be ended only by going forward or backward : each inconsistent nobleness being a fragment of discipleship, an accepted task of Sonship.

Relapse into the conscious animal is impossible. That means to choose chaos, darkness, death : the life of the self-wrapped creature whose eyes have not been opened is of God's appointment in its season. The times of that ignorance He foreordains. But it is gone ages ago past recall.   The brighter and more perfect future, the consummation of the kingdom of God is to be reached only through much tribulation. God is the Maker of it.   He has made it already in His Son.   We are His fellowworkers in bringing it to pass.

The goal determines the character of the way : its progress is always ⌐upward⌐.   It leaves nothing as an end to itself, acquiesces in nothing as remaining undirected to noble use.   It refuses to take the world as it stands as already good, but takes what is as the suggestion of what should be.

Distraction within is the way to make life useless and barren.

Obedience is the substance of all Sonship ; obedience accomplished in suffering is the substance of all present human sonship.

Abnegation is not itself the good, but the most universal condition for the human attainment of the good.

Christ promises not happiness but life : yet sometimes life through death : the right hand may have to be cut off, or the right eye plucked out.

We are slow to believe that the Cross of anguish can be a Tree of Life.

The old world was shaped by the intermediate groupings of mankind,—family race and nation. Christianity, taking up the tentative efforts of later times, established the two extremes in union, individualism and communism. Thus the single human being for the first time reaches his true dignity: but only in relation to the human race and to the Church, which is mankind knowing and fulfilling its destiny.

UNUS IGITUR DEUS PATER,...ET UNUS CHRISTUS JESUS DO-
MINUS NOSTER, VENIENS PER UNIVERSAM DISPOSITIONEM, ET
OMNIA IN SEMETIPSUM RECAPITULANS;...UTI, SICUT IN SUPER-
CAELESTIBUS ET SPIRITALIBUS ET INVISIBILIBUS PRINCEPS
EST VERBUM DEI, SIC ET IN VISIBILIBUS ET CORPORALIBUS
PRINCIPATUM HABEAT IN SEMETIPSUM PRIMATUM ASSUMENS,
ET APPONENS SEMETIPSUM CAPUT ECCLESIAE UNIVERSA
ATTRAHAT AD SEMETIPSUM APTO IN TEMPORE; NIHIL ENIM
INCOMTUM ATQUE INTEMPESTIVUM APUD EUM, QUOMODO
NEC INCONGRUENS EST APUD PATREM....OMNIA QUAE PRAE-
COGNITA ERANT A PATRE, ORDINE ET TEMPORE ET HORA
PRAECOGNITA ET APTA PERFECIT DOMINUS NOSTER, UNUS
QUIDEM ET IDEM EXISTENS, DIVES AUTEM ET MULTUS,
DIVITI ENIM ET MULTAE VOLUNTATI PATRIS DESERVIT.

ONE THEREFORE IS GOD, THE FATHER,...AND ONE IS
CHRIST JESUS, OUR LORD, COMING THROUGH THE ENTIRE
ECONOMY OF THINGS, AND GATHERING UP THE SUM OF
ALL THINGS INTO HIMSELF (Eph. i. 10);...THAT, AS IN THINGS
HEAVENLY AND SPIRITUAL AND INVISIBLE THE WORD OF
GOD IS SUPREME, SO ALSO IN THINGS VISIBLE AND CORPOREAL
HE MAY HAVE SUPREMACY, TAKING THE PRIMACY INTO HIM-
SELF (Col. i. 18), AND THAT PLACING HIMSELF AS HEAD TO
THE CHURCH (Eph. i. 22; Col. i. 18) HE MAY DRAW ALL THINGS
UNTO HIMSELF IN FITTING SEASON; FOR NOTHING IS DIS-
ORDERLY AND UNSEASONABLE WITH HIM, EVEN AS NOTHING
IS INHARMONIOUS WITH THE FATHER....ALL THINGS WHICH
HAD BEEN FOREKNOWN BY THE FATHER, OUR LORD ACCOM-
PLISHED IN FOREKNOWN AND FITTING ORDER AND SEASON
AND TIME, HE BEING IN HIS NATURE ONE AND THE SAME,
YET WITHAL RICH AND MANIFOLD, FOR HE SERVES THE
RICH AND MANIFOLD WILL OF THE FATHER.

IRENAEUS.

CAMBRIDGE: PRINTED BY C. J. CLAY, M.A. & SONS, AT THE UNIVERSITY PRESS.

For EU product safety concerns, contact us at Calle de José Abascal, 56–1°,
28003 Madrid, Spain or eugpsr@cambridge.org.

 www.ingramcontent.com/pod-product-compliance
Ingram Content Group UK Ltd.
Pitfield, Milton Keynes, MK11 3LW, UK
UKHW010343140625
459647UK00010B/780